RUGBYWORLD

Yearbook 2017

Editor

Ian Robertson

Photographs

Getty Images

Published in the UK in 2016 by
Lennard Publishing, an imprint of
Lennard Associates Ltd,
Mackerye End,
Harpenden, Herts AL5 5DR
email: orders@lennardqap.co.uk

Distributed by G2 Entertainment
c/o Orca Book Services
160 Eastern Avenue, Milton Park
Abingdon, OX14 4SB

ISBN: 978-1-78281-617-1

Production editor: Chris Marshall
Text and cover design: Paul Cooper

The publishers would like to thank Getty Images for providing most of the photographs for
this book. The publishers would also like to thank AIG, Fotosport UK, Fotosport Italy, Inpho
Photography, World Rugby, Chris Thau, Rhino Rugby, Charmaine Chitate and Wooden Spoon
for additional material.

Printed and bound in Italy
by L.E.G.O. S.p.A

We have a great sporting culture here at Norton Rose Fulbright, and we want to help make sure every child can enjoy sport. As rugby fans, we are particularly delighted to support Wooden Spoon through our corporate responsibility programme in London.

We believe that every child should have the chance to thrive in life, and so our charitable agenda across the whole of our legal practice focuses on improving opportunities for children and young people who are disadvantaged – whether physically, mentally or socially. I am proud to support Wooden Spoon, whose personal values so closely match our own.

Our focus is on local organisations where we feel we can make a real impact and benefit the communities in which we work. As well as providing funds for Wooden Spoon, we also encourage our people to participate in volunteering and fund-raising initiatives.

I wish everyone at Wooden Spoon a rewarding year ahead, and I would like to thank every person involved for their ongoing dedication and devotion to disadvantaged and disabled children in the UK.

Peter Martyr
Global Chief Executive
Norton Rose Fulbright

As the 2016/17 season gets underway, there is no doubt that this is a hugely exciting time to be associated with the game of rugby. Last season marked the sixth year of HSBC's sponsorship of the World Rugby Sevens Series, and it is fair to say that it was a truly ground breaking year. In the women's game it was our pleasure to be the first ever title sponsor of the Women's Series, as the women's game took another huge step forward.

All of this led to a pivotal moment for the sport, rugby's inclusion in the Olympic Games. We were extremely proud to see the stars of the World Rugby Sevens Series that we know and love compete on the biggest global stage. For HSBC the appeal of sevens rugby is clear. The World Series goes all over the world to some of the biggest rugby nations, but it also gives opportunities to some of rugby's fastest developing nations to grow their game on the world stage.

HSBC continues to invest in the present and future of rugby more broadly. Sevens is a great way to introduce young people to the game and we are proud to support the development of the next generation through sponsoring rugby festivals across the globe. We also partner with the world's largest schools sevens competition at Rosslyn Park. Away from Sevens, we are delighted to have extended our partnership with the Wallabies and we also continue to support Hong Kong men's and women's teams.

With the Olympics now complete on the back of a wildly successful 2015 Rugby World Cup, rugby is truly booming. With new growth and new opportunities, 2016/17 looks set to be the biggest ever season for rugby, and we can't wait to see it get started.

Giles Morgan
Global Head of Sponsorship and Events
HSBC Holdings plc

Fortune favours the brave

And the doggedly determined

There's ambition in all of us. At HSBC we're
here to support you in any way we can.

Proud supporter of the Wooden Spoon

Issued by HSBC Holdings plc.

Contents

NORTON ROSE FULBRIGHT

Where complex transactions require a confident approach, we're there.

A top legal brand, we have the industry understanding and global perspective needed to tackle the most complex challenges. Our service is cross-border and keenly commercial, and it is delivered by lawyers with deep industry knowledge. This means, we can help you make your next move with confidence.

Law around the world
nortonrosefulbright.com

Financial institutions | Energy | Infrastructure, mining and commodities

FOREWORD

by HRH THE PRINCESS ROYAL

BUCKINGHAM PALACE

HRH The Princess Royal,
Royal Patron of Wooden Spoon.

Wooden Spoon is motivated by its rugby heritage and with the continued support of its volunteers and the rugby community, the charity continues its important work to transform the lives of children and young people with a disability or facing disadvantage. As the children's charity of rugby, Wooden Spoon uses rugby to support a wide range of projects that are not just rugby focused. From sensory rooms, specialist playgrounds and sports activity areas to respite and medical centres and community based projects, the charity has funded 68 projects in last year, making a difference to 20,000 disabled and disadvantaged children and their families across the UK and Ireland.

Wooden Spoon's vision is that every child and young person, no matter what their background, has access to the same opportunities through the power of rugby. They have launched a new campaign to provide young people with disabilities better opportunities to become involved with Wheelchair Rugby. With Team GB Olympic and Paralympic role models demonstrating commitment for their chosen sports, Wooden Spoon recognises the opportunity to help more young people with a disability access the physical, social and emotional benefits of playing sport.

As Patron of Wooden Spoon I thank you for giving Wooden Spoon the ability to do so much for so many and wish you continued success in your fundraising activities.

Anne

WE ARE RUGBY.

Wooden Spoon
The children's charity of rugby

Love rugby?
Get involved

Together we can change children's lives through the power of rugby.

visit the website to find out more:

wswearerugby.org.uk   #wearerugby

Craig's story

Wooden Spoon
The children's charity of rugby

When Craig* was asked to leave home at 16 by his mum, his life was heading in a downhill direction. Craig's mum felt unable to cope, as Craig drifted further into spending time on the streets, taking drugs and hanging around with a bad crowd.

Placed in a children's home, Craig was feeling stuck in life. He was desperate for independence but couldn't see a way of being able to support himself. He became more frustrated and bitter about his future.

Thankfully, just when things were looking very bleak for Craig, he found crucial support through a special Wooden Spoon funded project – HITZ.

With their help, Craig was given the support he needed to develop a focus and learn life skills in order to support himself. The programme enabled him to get involved in education again, learn employability skills and boost his mood and self-esteem through rugby.

Craig secured himself a job with the local council; he now lives in his own accommodation and has a great support network. He has even started rebuilding a relationship with his mum.

The money you raise can help many young people living in desperate situations turn their lives around, and in turn, make a positive impact on society.

The money you raise can help many young people living in desperate situations turn their lives around, and in turn, make a positive impact on society.

*Names and specific circumstances have been changed to protect the identity of the young person.

Let's TRY and use the power of rugby to change children's lives

Hello, my name is Phil Vickery.

I am lead ambassador for Wooden Spoon. I'm passionate about the charity because I really believe that rugby can change children's and young peoples lives, and I want you to help us do more.

This year is going to be one of the most exciting for rugby in the UK and Ireland, we are celebrating the many things that the sport has given to all the people who have played it, supported it and been helped through it. We are using this opportunity to launch our 'We Are Rugby' campaign.

From cooking for your mates, to organising a race night at work, to co-ordinating your own rugby tournament at school or college, we are asking you to raise money and help make an incredible difference to disadvantaged and disabled children's lives across the UK and Ireland.

I have had the privilege to visit many of the projects Wooden Spoon supports. Someone who really sticks in my mind is Maxine* who had tragically lost her son, Archie* to a life-limiting condition.

Despite everything she had been through, Maxine was so thankful to us as a charity. With the accommodation we funded at the children's hospice where Archie was cared for, Maxine and her family were able to spend his last days all together.

She was so appreciative that, with our help, she was with her child in his final stages of life. That's the kind of life-changing support we can make happen.

So you see it doesn't matter what you do as long as you do something. This handy fundraising pack will help you raise as much as you can, and every penny helps change even more lives.

Thank you for everything you're about to do.

You're brilliant.

Phil Vickery

Inspired by our rugby heritage, we've been able to help over a million children and young people through our life-changing projects since we were founded in 1983.

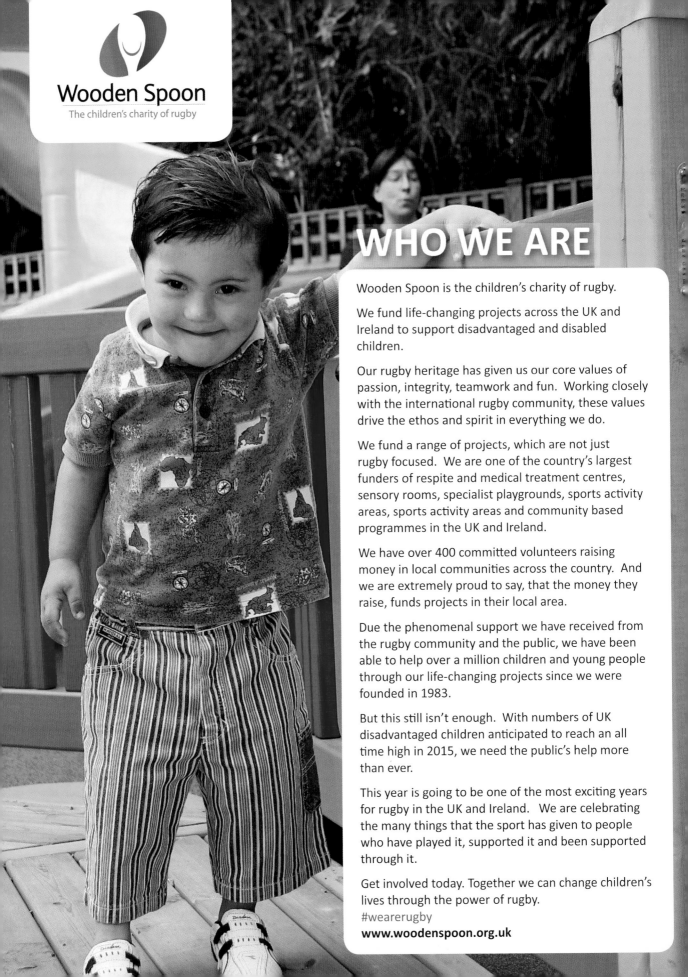

Wooden Spoon
The children's charity of rugby

WHO WE ARE

Wooden Spoon is the children's charity of rugby.

We fund life-changing projects across the UK and Ireland to support disadvantaged and disabled children.

Our rugby heritage has given us our core values of passion, integrity, teamwork and fun. Working closely with the international rugby community, these values drive the ethos and spirit in everything we do.

We fund a range of projects, which are not just rugby focused. We are one of the country's largest funders of respite and medical treatment centres, sensory rooms, specialist playgrounds, sports activity areas, sports activity areas and community based programmes in the UK and Ireland.

We have over 400 committed volunteers raising money in local communities across the country. And we are extremely proud to say, that the money they raise, funds projects in their local area.

Due the phenomenal support we have received from the rugby community and the public, we have been able to help over a million children and young people through our life-changing projects since we were founded in 1983.

But this still isn't enough. With numbers of UK disadvantaged children anticipated to reach an all time high in 2015, we need the public's help more than ever.

This year is going to be one of the most exciting years for rugby in the UK and Ireland. We are celebrating the many things that the sport has given to people who have played it, supported it and been supported through it.

Get involved today. Together we can change children's lives through the power of rugby.

#wearerugby

www.woodenspoon.org.uk

THE STORY BEHIND WOODEN SPOON

A wonderful legacy emerged in 1983 after five England rugby supporters went to Dublin to watch England in the final game of the Five Nations Championship against the Irish. The game was lost 25-15 and England finished last in the table with just a single point gained from their draw against Wales.

After the match, in a Dublin bar surrounded by celebrating Ireland supporters, the five England supporters sought some consolation only for three of their Irish friends to present them with a wooden spoon, wrapped in an Irish scarf on a silver platter as a memento of England's dismal season.

Accepting the gift with good humour and grace, the England fans resolved to hold a golf match to see who would have the honour of keeping the wooden spoon. Just a few months later the golf match was held and in the course of an entertaining day an astonishing sum of £8,450 was raised. The money was used to provide a new minibus for a local special needs school, Park School. This was to be the of first many Wooden Spoon charitable projects that has grown to over 600 in the years since.

From defeat on the rugby field, and a tongue-in-cheek consolation prize, the Wooden Spoon charity was born.

OUR ROYAL PATRON

Our Royal Patron is HRH The Princess Royal who gives generously of her time.

OUR RUGBY PATRONS

The IRFU, RFU, WRU, SRU, RFL all support us in our charitable work.

SPORTING PARTNERS

We work closely with a variety of clubs, league associations and governing bodies who help us achieve our vision of improving young lives though the power of rugby.

Buy a woolly hat!

Wooden Spoon
The children's charity of rugby

Chris Robshaw, Michael Owen, even Sir Ranulph Fiennes are wearing our wonderful woolly hats!

Don't miss out on your limited edition Wooden Spoon woolly hat.
Buy online at **woodenspoon.org.uk/woollyhat**

Sir Ranulph Fiennes

Alex Cuthbert

Michael Owen

Every woolly hat raises much needed funds for disabled and disadvantaged children and young people across the UK and Ireland.

COMMENT & FEATURES

The Welsh Regions
What Does the Future Hold?

by STEVE BALE

'But for this thing ever to work properly, there remains an overriding problem: the fundamental dichotomy between the Wales team and the four regional feeders'

ABOVE Scarlets, Wales's highest-finishing region in the 2015-16 PRO12, on the way to defeat in Galway against Connacht, the Irish 'Cinderella' province who won the title.

The Welsh regional sides, all four of them compared with the outsize 18 who used to form the pre-professional Merit Table, are given a persistently hard time by their opponents on the pitch and by their critics off it. It would help if they had had more than one qualifier, the Scarlets, for this season's European Champions Cup, or indeed if they had had a PRO12 semi-finalist. That would have to have been the Scarlets too, but their challenge faded to nothing like everyone else's.

These failures would by themselves make an easy target of the Scarlets, Ospreys, Blues and Dragons as a collective. But there are also issues of identity, or wider regional appeal, which particularly afflict the Dragons in Newport and Blues in Cardiff. Combine these various failings and there is too little clarity about how and when these institutions might secure the success – whether in trophies or indeed appealing to a wider public – that in turn would properly underwrite Wales's success.

There is an alternative view, though. For all the dispersal, or destruction, of loyalties that had stood for decades, the umbrella body Pro Rugby Wales (PRW) contends that between them the regions actually attract more support than all those 'senior' clubs had done for years.

'I am an engineer, so tend to work in facts and figures,' said Mark Davies, PRW's chief executive. 'I understand all the romance of the past. We all look with rose-tinted spectacles.

'But the consistent level of attendance, season tickets and commercial support from local businesses is vastly greater than it ever was at club level.

'We have to be realistic. We have four regions in a south Wales corridor with 1.9 million people. On that basis our attendance as a proportion of our available population will be considerably greater than any other country.'

Even if you disagree with Davies' assertion, or dismiss him as a partial witness, he is right to defend his regions' interests as effectively the only game in town for sub-international Welsh rugby. Unless the Welsh Rugby Union rip it all up and reboot the entire pro game in the Principality. Unlikely.

It is worth remembering that during Wales's years of high, if intermittent, achievement from the 2005 Grand Slam, every single one of their protagonists, including those who fetched up playing in France

BELOW Wales and Lions centre Jonathan Davies scores for Clermont Auvergne against Exeter Chiefs in the 2015-16 Champions Cup. Davies is back at Scarlets for 2016-17.

or England, came through the regional system. Some such as Jonathan Davies and Dan Lydiate even came back, and the WRU are pumping an ever-increasing flow of cash into the national dual contracts that have made this possible. This may not be a fair exchange, but for every emigrating Taulupe Faletau there is an immigrating Bradley Davies.

Here again is the worthy Mark Davies, whose experience previous to PRW includes being head of Honda's European motorcycles division as well as the Scarlets' chief executive: 'We are trying to run five competitive entities, four regions and one national side, out of a pro player base in Wales of just 200. The challenge for the regions is having the resources for the strength in depth needed across a long season if you are carrying a 25 per cent injury rate, and have the impact of call-ups for an international side, from just four clubs against, say, 12 in England or 14 in France.'

Davies makes a reasonable point even if it does lose something in the translation when we consider the drastic diminution of the France team at a time of unprecedented TV-derived wealth in the Top 14. Even the Irish, hitherto a standing rebuke for the Welsh, have started feeling the pinch. That said, Connacht's formidable achievement in winning the 2015-16 PRO12 shows how it can be done – the 'Cinderella' Irish province outgunning their better-heeled compatriots, all of whom are previous winners of this league. But all four of Connacht, Leinster, Ulster and Munster finished in the top six, so made Europe's elite competition. The Scarlets managed fifth, but the Blues, Ospreys and Dragons trailed in seventh, eighth and tenth. The excuse of international calls applies no less to the Irish than the Welsh.

At least in Ireland there is no identity problem, though those of us who used to attend, say, Pontypool's nondescript annual match against Munster in the 1980s would know there was nothing certain about the provincial rugby sides becoming the forces they eventually did. The Welsh regions have no such historical or cultural legitimacy. But what they do have is a powerful rugby heritage from the previous eminent clubs of Wales, Pontypool being one. There would be no logical reason for that project to fail but for the parochialism that once seemed to be a strength of Welsh rugby. You have only to consider the apparently insoluble difficulty Cardiff Blues have had in creating any affinity with the Valleys communities around Pontypridd – despite a major percentage of their players coming from that very area – to understand.

There again, this goes back to the very formation of regional rugby in 2003, when Cardiff were given stand-alone status to leave the Valleys represented by the Warriors' Bridgend/Pontypridd franchise. When this fifth region was disbanded after a solitary season, the mess was of the WRU's creation. For some it has never been cleaned up. The Valleys backbiting against the Blues, and against the Dragons from their Gwent hinterland including Pontypool for that matter, is strident and continuous; also deeply undermining when the Blues are supposed to represent a far wider area than just Cardiff, and the Dragons than Newport.

If there is hope that such divisions will ever be healed, perhaps it will come from the younger generation who have never known anything other than a regional set-up. Dan Biggar and Alun Wyn Jones, to take two obvious examples, are youngsters' heroes in Swansea – or Neath – because they are Ospreys, not All Whites or All Blacks. Swansea and Neath are no longer an unholy alliance.

But for this thing ever to work properly, there remains an overriding problem: the fundamental dichotomy between the Wales team and the four regional feeders, the grievance that the regions are forever undermined by the national team they serve. Every autumn and every New Year, off the international players go, leaving coaches such as the Ospreys' Steve Tandy to juggle with resources limited in number, diminished in age and depleted in experience. With a World Cup in 2015 as well, it was more than Tandy could withstand. Hence the Ospreys' appearance down in the European Challenge Cup for the very first time in their 14 seasons. 'We are proud of the number of guys we send to the national camp and want to continue making the substantial contribution we do,' Tandy said.

'But it does get harder every year with the players we bring in being younger and younger. Resources tend to mean we are getting thinner and thinner. They are coming through thick and fast but we have to get them coming through thicker and faster than ever.'

Last season, Test absences compounded by injuries, the Ospreys manifestly failed in Tandy's laudable endeavour. The notion that Wales may just have had some responsibility had never been properly articulated until Andrew Hore was departing as the Ospreys' chief executive. Lest we forget, professional Welsh rugby amounts to more than merely Wales, just like its amateur predecessor, though the prevalent, sardonic, description of Wales as 'the fifth region' plays into the narrative of everything deriving from the national team.

As he left the liabilities of the Liberty Stadium behind to take up a sunnier new life with the Waratahs in Sydney, across the Tasman from his native New Zealand, Hore begged to differ. 'We definitely need to stop looking at international rugby as the only income-generating part of the game,' he said.

'It's professional rugby as a whole that does that. All the regions have been successful in developing young players. It's good for our club to have internationals, but what makes us start to wonder whether it's worth it is when these guys are being thrashed week in week out.

'What people don't see is there is a lot of hurt in our game outside the national team that will ultimately be reflected in the national team.'

Hore had a specific objection to the fourth November Test the WRU annually shoehorn into the calendar. This wilfully helps undermine the regions' European prospects in order to generate revenue without regard to their stated ideal of 'player welfare', let alone regional welfare. But if the union can also take the money by agreeing an extra post-season Test at Twickenham – as they gratuitously did – then Andrew Hore and the hard-pressed regions in need of help not hindrance are preaching to the deaf.

PROUD PARTNER OF
WOODEN SPOON

GREENE KING IPA
THE PERFECT
MATCH PINT

'If You Build It ...'
Cleo and the Zimbabwe Academy
by DAVID STEWART

'It will help keep players around, groom them for national and club rugby, so these become competitive. A lot of players will have something to look forward to'

It is tempting to see Cleopas Makotose as a 21st-century Ray Kinsella, the character played in *Field of Dreams* by Kevin Costner, who when looking at his cornfield, hears a voice say, 'If you build it, he will come'. Swap a baseball diamond in Iowa for a rugby academy in Harare, and one gets an insight into the ambitious thinking of the former Zimbabwean captain.

Tonderai Chavhanga, Brian Mujati, Tendai ('the Beast') Mtawarira (all South Africa), Takudzwa Ngwenya (USA), David Denton (Scotland) and the great David Pocock (Australia) are current or recent

ABOVE Cleopas Makotose, a Zimbabwe international from 2003 to 2015, and skipper of the national side for five years from 2005, who is now trying to establish a rugby academy in his home country.

internationals. Leicester's Mike Williams and Exeter's Dave Ewers may be future English Test players. All are from Zimbabwe. So too were Bobby Skinstad, Adrian Garvey, Gary Teichmann, David Smith and the late Ian Robertson (all went south and became Springboks), while David Curtis followed his father Bryan into an Irish jersey. The country has long been a producer of rugby talent.

Makotose is another. He emerged from the famous Plumtree School in Matabeleland, which has produced Victor Olonga, another former national captain, and brother Henry, the Test cricketer. His debut for the Sables, as the national team is styled, was at home to Uganda in 2003 at inside centre. Cleo went on to earn most of his caps in midfield, forming a solid pairing with Daniel Hondo (later to become the Sables Sevens coach, and now a collaborator in the academy enterprise). Former coach Chris Lampard, who had spotted Cleo's leadership potential when in charge at Under 21 level, later appointed him as captain of the senior side in 2005, a role he held for the next five seasons. Brendan Dawson is one of his country's most capped players, and provides a link to the heady days of their participation in the 1991 World Cup. Under the coaching of the former back-row forward, and with Cleo a fixture in the side, they won the Africa Cup in 2012, and retained the tri-nations series title (involving Kenya and Uganda) in which the Sables had triumphed the previous year.

Enock Muchinjo, a local sports journalist, describes Makotose as 'known for his fierce patriotism and dedication to the national cause, a warrior through and through'. Those qualities drive his new ambition. Along with others in the local game, Cleo recognises that those leaving school are inadequately prepared for adult rugby compared with their contemporaries in South Africa or the UK. The introduction to his business plan recites, 'Most schoolboys do not persist after leaving because of a lack of opportunity domestically. We want to make the sport a better hobby, even a career option for more boys. An analysis of what made our recent Springboks excel gave birth to this project.' Dumile Moyo, former chairman of the national team fund-raising committee, said 'an academy is essential for the identification, nurturing and development of talent. Participants need access to professional seasoned coaches including visiting ones and enjoy specialised training like conditioning, defence, attack and other specialised skills.'

World Rugby are aware of the issue. Following a review of the progress made by Tier Two nations in the 2015 World Cup, Head of Competitions & Performance Mark Egan said, 'The three key pillars we invested in over the last four years were competition structure, high performance and coaching structures and strength and conditioning.' It is to be hoped this approach will now be adopted by the global governing body with the next tier of competing countries. One indication of faith from Egan's colleagues in the Zimbabwean game was the honour of hosting the World Rugby U20 Trophy (B Division) in April. Samoa beat Spain in sudden death in extra time of the final, thus securing promotion to the World Rugby U20 Championship, the A Division event, in 2017.

Economic and political conditions in the country have been far from ideal in recent years, but it is a shame the Zimbabwe Rugby Union have made little demonstrable progress in this area. Their website has a heading marked 'development', but clicking on it at any stage to date in 2016 reveals a blank page underneath. As assistant coach to the national women's Sevens, Cleo is still working inside the system, while pursuing the academy initiative independently.

The likes of Mtawarira and Mujati, contemporaries both, have been supportive. So too Gareth Jones, the former Western Province loose-head prop and now chairman of False Bay RFC in Cape Town, where Makotose played for a season. Cleo visited the UK in February 2016 seeking advice and investment. An overture to Reg Clark, managing director of Rhino, proved fruitful – he is now their representative for the south-central and East African region, providing a ready source of equipment and technical back-up. When Albert Pestana of Rhino Rugby South Africa visited he observed, 'Zimbabwe has the raw natural talent to compete very favourably at Fifteens and Sevens. I was impressed with the skills and tenacity when watching Under-17 and Under-18 trial matches at Chinhoyi.'

FACING PAGE Cleo with Albert Pestana of Rhino Rugby South Africa, who was impressed by the talent on display at trials matches he attended in Zimbabwe.

Noddy Kanyangarara, current ZRU vice-president and former national side manager, is in no doubt. 'An academy is key in Zim rugby though it has to start from the bottom [Under-13s] and build upwards. The structure of the schools season does not help with development, as kids just get to play rugby in the second term and move to other sports in the third and first terms. In an academy, they are kept together

training throughout the year and improving their skills and possibly getting game time. Those Under-13s will then move up the following year into Under-14s then the next batch comes through. Within four years you will develop talent that can filter into national teams.'

Dawson's successor and present Sables coach Cyprian Mandenge agrees. 'It will help keep players around, groom them for national and club rugby, so these become competitive. A lot of players will have something to look forward to. We need qualified coaches there, as at the moment we are having to teach some basics at national level.'

Cleo retired from international rugby in 2015, following wins over Kenya and Tunisia. He also represented his country with distinction in the Sevens arena. The connection with the award-winning film mentioned at the top of this article is not entirely coincidental. The playing career of Modreck Makotose, his elder brother, was cut short by a car accident in Bulawayo a week after his call-up to the national side. Modreck went on to become development manager of the ZRU, but died of malaria in 2012. The establishment of an effective and high-functioning academy would be a wonderful tribute to Cleo's late brother, and a tremendous shot in the arm for Zimbabwean rugby.

An On and Off Affair
Rugby and the Olympic Games

by CHRIS THAU

'In 1900, France, who selected a team from the Paris region captained by the legendary Frantz Reichel, became the first Olympic champions at rugby'

There is ample evidence that rugby, a game Baron Pierre de Coubertin had both preached and practised, was one of the favourite sports of the founder of the modern Olympics. The baron was in his early twenties when he visited Rugby School several times between 1883 and 1887. By that time rugby football was well established in the British Isles, and was making inroads among de Coubertin's young countrymen in a handful of clubs in Le Havre and Paris. The baron was a multifarious sporting talent engaged in boxing, fencing, rowing, horse-riding and, after his visits to Rugby, in 'football-rugby' as the game was called in France at the time. After his return from England, de Coubertin became an active promoter of physical education in general and 'football-rugby' in particular, which he managed to introduce into several schools in Paris, securing the long-term future of the game in France, which led to his induction into the World Rugby Hall of Fame in 2007. He went on playing rugby with his friends in the Bois de Boulogne and although there is no information about his prowess, his knowledge of the finer points of the game was well respected by his peers, who elected him to referee the inaugural French Championship final of 1892, between Stade Français and Racing Club de France.

ABOVE France, the first Olympic rugby champions, who beat a side from Germany and one from Great Britain to win the gold medal at the Paris Games of 1900.

In 1900, France, who selected a team from the Paris region captained by the legendary Frantz Reichel (one of de Coubertin's friends), became the first Olympic champions at rugby by beating Frankfurt (the club representing Germany) 27-17 and Moseley Wanderers (a selection from the Midlands clubs, which included several players from Moseley RFC, representing Britain) 27-8. The final match of the rugby tournament between Germany and Britain did not take place, because the Wanderers team had to return to England after their game against the French, which was played on a Sunday. The rugby matches drew big crowds and were afforded large press coverage.

ABOVE Baron Pierre de Coubertin, rugby enthusiast and founder of the modern Olympic Games, with rugby friends.

Not unexpectedly, the American organisers of the St. Louis Olympics chose American football rather than rugby as a demonstration sport in 1904, but the 1908 Games, held in London, brought rugby back into the Olympic programme. Great Britain were originally scheduled to meet France, with the winners taking on Australia, but one week before the match France withdrew on the grounds that they could not raise a representative team and the two remaining entrants, Australia, represented by a team selected from the touring Wallabies, and Great Britain, represented by English county champions Cornwall, met in the only match of the 1908 Games. The visitors, who fielded a very strong side including their youngest tourist, Daniel Carroll, destined to become rugby's first double Olympic gold medallist, demolished Cornwall 32-3.

Rugby was absent from the Olympic programme in 1912, but after the Great War it re-emerged as an Olympic sport at the 1920 Games in Antwerp. The Home Unions did not take part, arguing that the event held in September was too early in the season to enable the British to compete on equal terms with the other teams. The Romanians and Czechoslovakia withdrew at the last moment, which left the USA, represented by a team of Californian students, and France as the only two competitors. The US, coached by their former Wallaby outside half Daniel Carroll, surprised the French with the vigour of their game and the precision of their defensive work and won the match 8-0 and with it the Olympic title.

The Games of the VIII Olympiad commenced on 4 May 1924 and lasted nearly three months, with the closing ceremony taking place on 27 July. Among the 3092 athletes from 44 countries competing in 17 sports, there were some 60 rugby players representing the reigning Olympic champions, the USA, the hosts France and newcomers Romania.

There was a huge gap in terms of ability and experience between the French, captained by their veteran No. 8 René Lasserre of Grenoble, who had made his international debut before the Great War ten years earlier, and the inexperienced Romanians, captained by their ageing centre-threequarter Nicolae Marascu, one of the pioneers of the game in the country. Not unexpectedly, the French despatched the newcomers from Eastern Europe by a record 61 points to 3 margin – according to some sources the score was actually 59-3 – scoring a record 13 tries in the process, including four by their famous winger Adolphe Jauréguy. On the following Sunday, 11 May, the US, captained by full back Charlie Doe, an Olympic gold medallist in 1920, comprehensively defeated Romania 37-0. The vocal French crowd supported Romania, who although they gave a good account of themselves were thoroughly outplayed by their bigger, faster, stronger and, to the surprise of the French, more skilful opponents. The defeat ended Romania's campaign in the Olympics but secured them the bronze, their first ever Olympic medal.

The Olympic final, like the first two games, was played at Stade Colombes in Paris – on 18 May 1924, before a strongly partisan crowd of about 50,000. The exceedingly generous odds of the local bookmakers, five to one for a straight French win, reflected the general state of euphoria in the aftermath of the Romanian game and no doubt influenced the mindset of the French team.

The US captain was No. 8 Colby Slater, an alumnus of California University (Davis), alongside Doe one of the several 1920 gold medallists in the US squad, while his opposite number was once again René Lasserre of FC Grenoble. The match was refereed by Albert Freethy of Wales, helped by the French Federation's secretary for international affairs, Cyril Rutherford, and Norman Slater, the brother of US skipper Colby, as touch judges.

While in the first half the French seemed able to absorb nearly everything the Americans threw at them, after the break and reduced to 14 men following Jauréguy's injury, the French defence eventually crumbled. The Americans added four more tries to their 3-0 half-time lead, with Henri Galau scoring France's solitary try, for a final scoreline of 17-3. The crowd went wild and the match ended in pandemonium, with the public throwing stones and bottles at the American players and with one of the US reserve players, Gideon Nelson, flattened by a walking stick.

Until 2016, this was the last time rugby featured in the programme of the modern Olympics, and for a variety of reasons all attempts to relaunch it as an Olympic sport failed. De Coubertin resigned as International Olympic Committee (IOC) president in 1925, and his successor, the Belgian Count Henri de Baillet-Latour, did not share the fondness of the founder for team sports in general and 'football-rugby' in particular. Rugby was never again part of the Olympics, though in May 1936 the newly formed Fédération Internationale de Rugby Amateur (FIRA) organised with the help of the German Rugby Federation (DRV) a pre-Olympic rugby tournament in Berlin and Hamburg. In the final, France defeated Germany 19-14 to win the gold medal, while Italy beat Romania 8-7 to capture the bronze.

Other than a couple of feeble attempts to have rugby included in the 1980 and 1988 Olympics by the hosts USSR and Korea respectively, the game's hierarchy remained largely unmoved by the Olympic option. The earliest serious attempts to ignite rugby's gradual return to the Olympic fold started during the early 1990s, with a series of informal meetings between the then IRFB general secretary, Keith Rowlands, and the British Olympic Association general secretary, Dick Palmer. A number of obstacles had to be overcome, including an application by the Paris-based FIRA to be accepted as an IOC member, as well as a feeling among influential members of the IRFB that rugby would have little to benefit from an association with the Olympics.

It was the nomination of the late Vernon Pugh of Wales as chairman of the IRFB in 1994 that hastened the game's advance towards renewed Olympic status. Pugh convinced the IRFB Council that Olympic membership – initially as a non-participation sport – would help bring rugby into the

Your *nest egg* could become a valuable source of income PROFITS.

Fig. 1:
An ordinary nest egg

Fig. 2:
A more valuable nest egg

FOR YEARS, cracking open your retirement nest egg and converting it into an annuity was your only option. But following the changes in the law last year, you can now fashion your nest egg into a valuable source of income Profits. Of course few know more about these gems than the Artemis hunters. We have expertise in income both at home and abroad. From both bonds and equities. And in each case, our hunters have a glittering reputation. The decision to access your pension savings is an extremely important one. Before you do so, Artemis strongly advises you to seek advice from a financial adviser to help you to understand your options. Please remember that past performance should not be seen as a guide to future performance. The value of an investment and any income from it can fall as well as rise as a result of market and currency fluctuations and you may not get back the amount originally invested.

ARTEMIS
The PROFIT Hunter

0800 092 2051   investorsupport@artemisfunds.com   artemis.co.uk

world family of sports and offer many of the smaller IRFB member unions an elevated status as members of their National Olympic Committees as well as additional funding. The first step towards Olympic membership was a low-key ceremony held in Cardiff in November 1994, when rugby applied to be accepted into the Olympic fold as a non-participation sport. The guests of the IRFB included the then IOC president, Juan Antonio Samaranch, and Jacques Rogge, a future president and a former Belgian rugby international. In his address Samaranch pointed out that rugby's history and values were very much in tune with the Olympic philosophy and traditions. In his reply Pugh said that the relationship between the game of rugby and the Olympics had commenced more than a century before, when the founder of the modern Olympic Games, Baron Pierre de Coubertin, visited Rugby School and developed an interest in the game.

The historic meeting in Cardiff was followed by a series of delicate negotiations with the IOC, led by Pugh, and after his untimely death, by his successors Dr Syd Millar of Ireland and Bernard Lapasset of France. On the technical side, the IRFB (IRB from 1998; now World Rugby) had offered the IOC the option of choosing between Fifteens and Sevens, presenting comprehensive submissions for separate 15-a-side and seven-a-side tournaments. At the same time the IRB led an increasingly vigorous campaign of expanding the Sevens game to a global audience and prominence, to match the exposure of the main game. In retrospect, one could argue that the launch of the IRB Sevens Series in 1999-2000 was the first step in getting Sevens on an Olympic path.

This rapid and controlled growth reflected the growing awareness and support for the short game within the Olympic Movement, which resulted in 2011 in a recommendation from the Olympic Programme Commission to the IOC Session to have Sevens included in the 2008 Beijing Games. The Olympic Programme Commission felt that the fast and spectacular game of Sevens was best suited to the multi-sport environment of the Olympics, as proven by its success in both the Commonwealth and Asian Games. Unfortunately the recommended changes to the Olympic programme were not carried through. In 2004 rugby was shortlisted for Olympic inclusion in 2012, which was a major breakthrough, but the 2005 IOC vote went to karate and squash. In the end, at the 2009 IOC Session in Copenhagen, the overwhelming majority of the participants voted in favour of rugby Sevens joining the Olympic programme at the 2016 Rio Olympics. After a break of 92 years rugby was back in the Olympics.

BELOW The US gold medallists from the 1920 Games in Antwerp. The Americans returned to win again in 1924 and remained Olympic champions until 2016.

ÉQUIPE NATIONALE DES ÉTATS-UNIS D'AMÉRIQUE
Champions des Olympiades d'Anvers

Squaring the Circle
Towards a Global Season?

by CHRIS FOY

'Attempts to align the north and south have been on the agenda since the dawn of professionalism, but the matter is now more pressing than ever before'

Bill Beaumont has an almighty task on his hands, at the start of his tenure as chairman of World Rugby. The debate over a global season concept has been simmering for years, but now the spectre of division and revolution looms large. This thorny issue is unlikely to be resolved over a pint or two in a Glasgow pub, as was the case back in 1999, when Beaumont took an old-school approach to averting the threat of an English exile from the Six Nations. This is a far more

complex test of the former Lions lock's diplomacy, with profound implications for the sport in both hemispheres. Attempts to align the north and south have been on the agenda since the dawn of professionalism, but the matter is now more pressing than ever before. In 2019, the current agreement governing international fixtures expires, and the doomsday scenario is that failure to conclude a new deal will lead to a schism between feuding factions.

New Zealand are leading a challenge to the status quo, founded primarily on concerns over financial imbalance. On the field, the south continues to dominate, despite Europe's greater commercial clout which has led to a mass migration of leading Kiwis, Australians and South Africans, as well as countless Pacific Islanders. The NZRU have set their stall out to indulge in a high-stakes game of brinkmanship, insisting that they will operate independently of World Rugby in arranging their own fixtures from 2020, if their calls for a global season are not met. Steve Tew, the union's chief executive, is prepared to use the All Blacks as the ultimate trump card.

Officials from New Zealand alerted their European counterparts during the summer about their stance and the debate was due to be discussed in earnest at World Rugby committee meetings in September. Tew had already made clear that he hoped Beaumont would set a positive tone, saying: 'We expect him [Beaumont] to show some leadership in that area.'

Outlining the potential ramifications if talks do not progress, Tew added: 'We don't believe the current system is sustainable. We need a different season structure than we have now and we're going to force that issue.

'The north can't do without the south at the international level and vice versa. If we can't get an agreement that is satisfactory then we will talk about playing among our southern-hemisphere colleagues a bit more.

'If that was the case, then ultimately there would be no window for a Lions series or a World Cup. No one wants that kind of chaos and I am 99 per cent sure we would not get to that point. We want to make sure the Lions series survives in whatever new calendar we have. We can make some adjustments for that.'

This willingness to be flexible when it comes to accommodating Lions tours reflects the focus on the bottom line of vital profits for the southern unions. Australia have been beset by financial problems, Argentina are still developing a professional infrastructure to support the rise of the Pumas and even New Zealand – for all their success and national passion for the sport – are operating with modest resources, compared to northern rivals.

Tew's hard-line approach has been backed by the All Blacks head coach, Steve Hansen, who spoke out before The Rugby Championship, saying: 'Tewie is on the money. If we organise our own games, I'm sure we'll get plenty of northern-hemisphere takers who will play us. They fill their stadiums when we play and make a lot of money.'

LEFT New World Rugby chairman former England captain Bill Beaumont (left) and his vice-chairman, ex-Puma skipper Agustín Pichot, have a job on their hands to satisfy the various parties' preferences regarding the global season concept.

Addressing the global season concept, Hansen – who has an understanding of both sides of the debate, having previously spent time coaching Wales – added: 'It just needs a willingness for everyone to look at it. Everyone will have to make slight adjustments. Just because the England CEO said, "Why do we need to change?", I wouldn't read that there isn't a growing desire to actually have a global season. We just need to get the right people in the room with the right mindset.'

Hansen was referring to the counter-argument raised by Ian Ritchie, the chief executive of the RFU, who has spoken out firmly in favour of the status quo, based on the old adage that – in financial terms at least – if it ain't broke, don't fix it. As the head of the world's richest union, his opinion carries major significance. 'With the Six Nations, the date in the calendar works well,' said Ritchie. 'As far as we're concerned, we have a great TV deal and stadia that are filled for every game. Why would you want to change something that works really well? So I can't see there being any significant move in that and the Autumn Internationals work terribly well for us as well. There have been a number of preliminary discussions about the global season. It's a priority moving on.'

Beaumont was, until recently, working closely with Ritchie as chairman of the RFU, prior to taking on the same senior role with World Rugby. Once his appointment was confirmed in May, he set his stall out to tackle the unruly mess of a worldwide calendar which is disjointed and overcrowded. In the interests of furthering that objective, Beaumont made it clear that shifting the Six Nations to a later date in the year would have to be considered. 'The game has changed and you have to keep moving,' he said. 'I think you have to be prepared to look at it [moving the Six Nations]. That could well be a solution. Everybody has to take a look at it. It's a question of compromise.'

The problem is that very few of those in the various corridors of power have shown much willingness to compromise when it comes to this awkward subject. Self-interest rules. New Zealand and other southern unions have championed the need for reform, but of course they expect the north to fall into line with their season, rather than vice versa. On the flip side, the English stance reflects a European conviction that their lucrative 'product' doesn't need to be altered. To further complicate the equation, the French and English clubs wield considerable power and may not take kindly to being told they have to make the historic leap to summer rugby, in order to enhance the game thousands of miles away.

Beaumont's World Rugby vice-chairman, the charismatic and combative Agustín Pichot, said after being elected: 'There are only really two big problems at the moment, it is the French league and the English league. You have two big markets [for club rugby] and the rest is driven by international rugby. You have to offer the clubs something better.'

While so much of the negotiating process will concentrate on what model would best drive revenue and profit all round, the other underlying factor is player welfare. Put simply, too much rugby is being played. A fully integrated global season would allow a streamlining of the calendar and, in turn, a reduction in the punishing workload for those at the sharp end of the club and Test game. That would chime with all the talk of tackling the concussion crisis which has stalked this tough, fiercely physical sport. Yet, while officials line up to preach about the importance of participants' health and safety, every league and union seeks to expand, rather than contract.

Perhaps the powerful French and English clubs would embrace the concept of aligning with the southern season if it allowed them to advance the much-touted prospect of a world club championship. That would also potentially open up the prospect of exploring new markets, such as the United States, which present so many commercial opportunities.

But if there is to be a global season, there must be compromise and a willingness to see the bigger picture. Somewhere, turkeys must vote for Christmas, by putting the greater good above their own self-interest, their own short-term profit, their own political agendas.

Conditions surely dictate that the notion of playing through a southern summer, with extreme heat in much of Australia and South Africa in particular, is unthinkable. On that basis alone, it makes more sense to explore a northern shift, to allow the global campaign to run from February to late November. As Beaumont has already suggested, the Six Nations could switch to April-May, with tours to the south in July and the same November encounters in Europe as there are at present.

Beyond that, fine-tuning the club calendar will take much will and work, but it could be done. In the rival code, Super League moved to summer and it has seemingly enhanced the competition. Matches in southern France and Italy may need to kick off in late evening, but pitches could be easily treated to prevent surfaces being too hard, with the associated threat of injury.

Those in favour of the status quo raise the alarm about clashing with cricket, football World Cups and the Olympics, but the current season runs parallel to European football's annual club campaigns. Frankly, only the most one-eyed of traditionalists would lament the loss of midwinter mudbaths and frozen conditions leading to cancellations.

Put aside self-interest and this is a monumental matter for rugby to address and resolve – urgently. All nations, however far apart, need each other to collectively safeguard and nurture a viable, vibrant, competitive sport into the future – while seeking long-term solutions to the financial and player-welfare factors which are driving this debate.

Brinkmanship is a dangerous game, but maybe it is necessary to bring about vital change. To do nothing is tantamount to wanton neglect. Something has to give. If Beaumont – aided and abetted by Pichot and leading officials worldwide – can bring the factions together and find a solution, it would represent an epic feat of statesmanship. Rugby cannot keep muddling through, in spite of the archaic system, rather than because of it.

BELOW A global campaign running from February to late November would mean less of the inclement weather and conditions for northern players.

next

ARE PROUD TO SUPPORT

THE WOODEN SPOON 2017

INTERNATIONAL SCENE

Generation Next
the New All Black Heroes

by RAECHELLE INMAN

'After New Zealand's 3-0 series whitewash over Wales in June 2016, Welsh captain Sam Warburton tweeted, "The depth of New Zealand's talent is frightening." And he is right'

When five All Black stars retired after the 2015 World Cup final the rest of the rugby world breathed a collective sigh of relief. New Zealand captain Richie McCaw led the exit along with fellow legends Dan Carter, Ma'a Nonu, Keven Mealamu and Conrad Smith.

But despite losing so much experience the All Blacks never really look weak because of their incredible depth. After New Zealand's 3-0 series whitewash over Wales in June 2016, Welsh captain Sam Warburton tweeted, 'The depth of New Zealand's talent is frightening.' And he is right.

Although not filling the gap left by one of the five retiring legends, Aaron Smith is headlining the new group, who are making a real mark on world rugby in the aftermath of the exit of the 'Big Five'. After being signed for Super Rugby in 2011, he became the Highlanders' first-choice No. 9 in 2012 and was also selected for the All Blacks that same year, making his debut in the iconic black jersey against Ireland. Smith's trademark bullet pass and fast-paced style suited the All Blacks' expansive game and he cemented his position in the starting team in 2013.

A skilful distributor and reader of the play, Smith has become an integral part of both the Highlanders and All Blacks and his exceptional form throughout 2015 led to him being nominated in two categories at the 2015 New Zealand Rugby Awards: Tom French Memorial Maori Player of the Year and Super Rugby Player of the Year. He was a stand-out player for the Highlanders in 2015, helping the team to their inaugural Super Rugby title. He bolstered his reputation, and, following consistent performances in the decisive series win over Wales in 2016, he is widely regarded as the best scrum half in the world.

Prior to the Welsh series, Smith signed with New Zealand Rugby and the Highlanders through to the end of the 2019 season. Smith said: 'I'm really excited and thankful for the commitment shown from New Zealand Rugby, including the Highlanders and Manawatu Turbos. Knowing I'm contracted for the next four years allows me to focus on my rugby and there are some exciting challenges ahead for the All Blacks which I hope to be part of.'

All Blacks coach Steve Hansen said: 'It's outstanding news for Aaron and for the All Blacks. With a number of senior players leaving at the end of this year, Aaron and other players will play a key role in the team as we face the exciting challenges coming up over that period, including the British & Irish Lions tour of New Zealand in 2017. We look forward to working with him.'

In the backs New Zealand have never had a shortage of talent. Losing two incredibly capable centres in Ma'a Nonu and Conrad Smith left a sizeable void. At the start of the 2016 Test series Steve Hansen picked Ryan

LEFT Three of the new generation of All Blacks – Sam Cane, Nehe Milner-Skudder and Aaron Smith – line up ahead of the RWC 2015 New Zealand v Argentina encounter at Wembley.

Crotty at inside centre and Tongan-born Malakai Fekitoa at outside. Fekitoa combines powerful running and abrasive defence in a potentially devastating package, just as Nonu used to. The All Blacks selectors first came calling in 2014 and Fekitoa concluded the year with eight Test caps and two tries. Remarkably, his elevation to the All Blacks came just four months after the explosive midfielder entered Super Rugby. After helping the Highlanders to their first ever Super Rugby title, Fekitoa played five Tests in 2015 and scored two tries at that year's World Cup.

At 25 years of age, fast and powerful winger Waisake Naholo already has six Tests and four international tries under his belt. Fijian-born Naholo demolished Wales in the 2016 matches, steamrolling over them. He made his All Blacks debut against Argentina in 2015, unfortunately injuring his leg in the same match, but recovered in time to play two matches at the Rugby World Cup in 2015. Injury again limited his time on the field during the 2016 Super Rugby series, but when he did appear, he showed all of his trademark pace and brilliance.

The formidable line breaker made his provincial debut in 2009 and was selected in the New Zealand Under 20 side for the Junior World Championship in 2011. The next year Naholo was called into the All Blacks Sevens squad. In 2014, he played in every match for Taranaki and scored nine tries as the team claimed the ITM Cup Premiership. The Highlanders snapped the winger up for the

2015 season and he thrived, helping the team to its first title. He was also one of the competition's top try scorers. If Naholo can remain injury-free he will be a powerhouse for New Zealand over the years ahead.

Chiefs full back Damian McKenzie, 21, has quickly become known for his big smile every time he steps up to kick a goal. However, it is his ability to create something out of nothing and his enormous courage which have attracted most attention. The Chiefs got their 2016 Super Rugby campaign off to a great start in Christchurch, beating the Crusaders, and everyone was talking about McKenzie, who made a hugely impressive tackle on gigantic Fijian winger Nemani Nadolo. It defied belief, as he lined him up, got low and not only saved a near certain try but bumped the giant winger into touch with perfect timing. When you consider that McKenzie weighs around 80kg (12st 8lb), and Nadolo around 130kg (20st 7lb), this tackle sums him up.

'Obviously we are pretty fortunate with Damian at the back,' said Chiefs coach Dave Rennie after that match. 'He is pretty keen to jump in behind the forwards to play off them, or jump into first receiver.

'I thought he was massive; he was an absolute handful and is just so electric. We were rapt with him. When guys are tiring, too, he is so quick and he is positive. So he found quite a bit of space, when the ball is kicking back. He played a big part in the last couple of tries, so it was great.'

All Black regular Aaron Cruden backed his Chiefs team-mate for an All Blacks call-up this year and McKenzie was rewarded with a place in the 2016 squad. 'He's got a really positive mindset in the way that he plays, and he really trusts his skill set and understands what he can do on the rugby field. And to have a guy like that out the back that, you know, can just create something out of almost nothing, it just really gets us as a team on the front foot and moving forward, and that's great,' Cruden said.

FACING PAGE All Black centre Malakai Fekitoa on duty for the Highlanders against the Hurricanes during Super Rugby 2016.

BELOW Chiefs full back Damian McKenzie produces his trademark smile as he lines up a kick at goal against the Crusaders in Christchurch. McKenzie has been included in the All Blacks squad but has yet to appear in a Test.

But he added that what makes the diminutive youngster different is his maturity and temperament. 'He's aware of the hype and the attention that could potentially become a distraction ... but he's a real sharp young man and he sort of doesn't let that stuff get on top of him.

'And you know I think he'll just continue to grow in the years to come.'

Not yet in the All Blacks squad, Richie Mo'unga, at 22 years of age, is another of the new breed of New Zealand players with real potential. He debuted for Canterbury in the ITM Cup during the 2013 season, his first year out of school. He impressed with a 27-point haul (a try, eight conversions and two penalties) in his first game, taking the man-of-the-match honours, and was named in the official squad for the first time in 2014.

BELOW Hooker Dane Coles, whose 'strength, mobility and speed have helped to redefine the qualities required for a modern international front-rower'. Here he is scoring against Georgia during the 2015 Rugby World Cup.

After selection in the New Zealand Under 20 squad for the IRB Junior World Championship in 2014, Mo'unga was selected for the Crusaders Wider Training Group in 2015. He was promoted to the full Crusaders squad for the 2016 Super Rugby season. While first five-eighth is his usual position, Mo'unga has the versatility to also play at full back. Wearing the coveted No. 10 jersey for the Crusaders, vacated by the phenomenal Dan Carter, has been like a dream come true for Mo'unga. 'I love it. It's like Disneyland for me, I am from Christchurch, born and raised here. I am living the dream, having a blast.'

Rugby is a 23-man game and the All Blacks really use the eight players on the bench well. They have the ability to seamlessly reshuffle the back line. Many of the reserves are multitaskers and are used cleverly as effective substitutions.

Another name to look for in the near future is Nehe Milner-Skudder, an impressive young All Black winger. In 2015 he made his debut, was named World Rugby Breakthrough Player of the Year and scored a try in the World Cup final. Despite being sidelined with injury in 2016, this youthful outside back will surely return to the All Black jersey when back to full fitness.

In the forwards, Richie McCaw's departure has the potential to leave the biggest gap. Loose forward Sam Cane is being touted as the heir apparent to McCaw, but the jury is still out. His work rate is not disputed; however, he has big shoes to fill.

Cane made his Super Rugby debut in 2010 at the tender age of 18. He has been a key part of the Chiefs team that won two Super Rugby titles, in 2012 and 2013. He first pulled on an All Black jersey at 20 and is seen to have leadership potential, having been included in the national side's leadership group in 2013, which is rare for a player who is not regularly in the starting XV.

Cane appeared in eight Test matches in 2015 and featured in the All Blacks side for the Welsh contests in 2016. His ill discipline, giving away penalties, raised a few eyebrows in New Zealand rugby circles. He has strong potential and the rugby world will watch with interest to see how he matures as an international.

Another dynamic loose forward, Liam Squire, debuted off the bench in 2016 in the final Test against Wales. He played his first Super Rugby season for the Chiefs in 2014. This marked a remarkable recovery for a player who had suffered a fractured spine three years previously. He had a solid season with the Chiefs, appearing 11 times. Squire moved from the Chiefs to the Highlanders in 2016. His power, size, mobility and impressive line-out skills caught the attention of the All Blacks selectors and his ball-carrying was strong on debut.

In 2015, Dane Coles cemented his place as the All Blacks first-choice hooker and started in the Rugby World Cup final victory over Australia. Coles's status as a leader was also recognised when he was named as captain of the Hurricanes for the 2016 Super Rugby season. Keven Mealamu was a rock at hooker for the All Blacks, chalking up 133 caps and surviving four World Cups. Coles is excelling in his role; his strength, mobility and speed have helped to redefine the qualities required for a modern international front-rower. He has an ability to break through tackles and flat-foot defenders that sets him apart. He is a fan favourite for Wellington and the Hurricanes, where he leads from the front.

Whilst the rest of the rugby world hoped the loss of five high-profile All Blacks would create a level playing field, New Zealand's impressive clean sweep of Wales clearly demonstrates the immense depth of talent in the Land of the Long White Cloud and signals a seamless continuation of dominance.

England's in England
the World Rugby U20 Championship
by ALAN LORIMER

'It was a style of rugby made for the likes of centre Marchant and flanker Will Evans, two players who, along with man of the final Mallinder, stamped their mark on the tournament'

Saturday 25 June 2016 will surely be a day to remember in English rugby history, as England's next generation of young stars won a third World Rugby U20 Championship title in Manchester just hours after Eddie Jones's senior team had completed a 3-0 series whitewash against Australia. This was the first World Rugby U20 Championship hosted by England and in the event the home side used Manchester to showcase the future of the English game. And it looks a good future. England were the outstanding side in the tournament, confirming their top status with a dominant display against Ireland in the final at the AJ Bell Stadium to finish winners by 45-21.

Remarkably England's world championship success in Manchester came only three months after the young Englishmen had finished a lowly fifth in the Under 20 Six Nations, their only victory having been against Italy. So how was such a massive turnaround achieved? For a start the RFU appointed a new coach in the former England and Bath forward Martin Haag at the end of the Six Nations to effect a change of mindset and to instil a new sense of belief in his young charges. The other important factor was the inclusion in the squad of a number of Premiership and Championship players, who had not been released by their clubs for the Six Nations, and none more influential than the Northampton Saints young star and England Under 20 captain, Harry Mallinder.

At 195cm (6ft 5in) and 105kg (16st 7lb) the Rugby School alumnus has a formidable physical presence, which most teams would happily utilise in their forward pack. Mallinder, however, was played at fly half, rather than his club position of centre or full back, and in the event it provided a winning formula for England. In the final against Ireland Mallinder accounted for over half of his side's points with a tally of two tries, five conversions and a penalty goal. England's other tries came from

RIGHT England Under 20 captain Harry Mallinder receives the World Rugby U20 Championship trophy from Bill Beaumont after his side's 45-21 win over Ireland Under 20 in the final.

the quick-footed centre Joe Marchant (2), the Newcastle No. 8 Callum Chick and the Worcester Warriors second-row Huw Taylor. For Ireland, who trailed 21-0 at the break, hooker Adam McBurney led the second-half fightback with a try, centre Shane Daly followed with a second Irish score made by a wonderful run out of defence by Jacob Stockdale and then No. 8 Max Deegan added a third touchdown.

What made England popular winners was their attractive style of rugby. Gone were the bulldozing tactics of yesteryear, when endless rolling mauls bored their opponents into submission, and in its place a premium package of running rugby and accurate handling with the emphasis on ball carriers putting support runners into space rather than seeking collisions.

Speaking after the final against Ireland Haag said: 'I thought the way we adapted and turned defence into attack was brilliant. We played with high intensity ... We're in a good place, the first-half performance was electric to watch. That's how these guys want to play – they want to play an exciting brand of rugby.'

It was a style of rugby made for the likes of Marchant and flanker Will Evans, two players who, along with man of the final Mallinder, stamped their mark on a tournament in which England emerged from the pool stage as the number one seeds after defeating Italy and Scotland, both by big scores, and then Australia.

It was perhaps good fortune for England that New Zealand were seeded fifth after the pool stage and not fourth. Had the Baby Blacks finished fourth then they would have played England in the semi-finals. Such a scenario, however, was thwarted in the final round of pool games by Wales limiting New Zealand to just two tries, thereby denying the Baby Blacks a bonus point, and by South Africa scoring five tries against France, resulting in the Baby Boks securing the fourth ranking.

In the semi-final against South Africa at the Manchester City Academy Stadium, England again demonstrated their title-winning credentials with a 39-17 victory in a match that was in the bag by

half-time. The other penultimate-round match also produced a convincing scoreline, Ireland winning 37-7 against Argentina.

Championship success for England should not have come as any surprise. It was essentially about tapping into and realising the potential of the large numbers involved in a high-quality Premiership and Championship academy system that gives young players skills training, expert strength-and-conditioning programmes, exposure to high-level competition and many of the other benefits of being in a professional rugby environment. Such a strong base of players and a core who have performed at senior level is a necessary if not a sufficient condition for success in the World Rugby U20 Championship. All 28 players in a squad have to be of a high standard, as indeed should be those on the stand-by list.

Yet Ireland, with considerably smaller numbers from which to select, still achieved heroics in the 2016 championship, the runners-up place representing their highest finishing position in the global tournament. While Ireland had some outstanding players likely to be capped at senior level in the next few years, their strength in depth was not that of England and therein lay much of the difference. Ireland's success will be measured not so much in terms of finishing second but more about bringing through the next generation of international players. In which context, full back Stockdale, who has already made appearances for Ulster, winger Hugo Keenan, No. 8 Deegan, named as the Player of the Tournament, second-row James Ryan, hooker McBurney and prop Andrew Porter could well figure in the Rugby World Cup.

Notwithstanding England's skilful and stylish title-winning performance, Ireland's inability to reproduce their earlier form in the final may have had much to do with the effort expended in the pool stage where the Irish faced tougher opponents than those in England's pool. First up for Ireland were Wales, the match resulting in a 26-25 win after the Irish had trailed 17-0 early on. Then there was Ireland's remarkable and tournament-defining 33-24 victory against New Zealand and finally a pool-winning 35-7 result against a Georgia side that proved difficult opponents for most teams.

It was not only Ireland who rose above their seeding. Argentina came into the tournament ranked ninth, but in the opening pool match Los Pumitas chewed up France to create the first shock of the day. Then against South Africa, the young Argentinians took another important scalp with a 19-13 victory over the Baby Boks; and when they defeated Japan, Argentina had earned themselves a place in the semi-finals.

Although Argentina were beaten by Ireland in the semi-finals, in the third-place play-off the young Pumas rediscovered their winning formula to defeat South Africa. It was a fitting ending for Argentina, who had played some glorious rugby and revealed future stars such as fly half Domingo Miotti, a world-class goal-kicker and a clever playmaker, and the centre and captain Juan Cruz Mallia, who scored a hat-trick against the Baby Boks.

For South Africa, 2016 marked a change in style from bulk forward play to a fast running game that recruited Sevens skills from the likes of their 18-year-old fly half Immanuel Libbok, full back Curwin Bosch and winger Edwill van der Merwe, surely the quickest player in the tournament.

Finishing one place behind South Africa were New Zealand. The Baby Blacks met their match against Ireland and came desperately close to losing against Wales, a 79th-minute penalty giving New Zealand an 18-17 win over the Welsh side. But a week later when the two sides met again, this time in the fifth-place semi-finals, New Zealand were a different force, seemingly on a mission to expunge from their collective memory two difficult games in the pool stage. In the event New Zealand cut loose to achieve a 71-12 victory over a Welsh side that could not live with the pace and handling skills of the Baby Blacks.

New Zealand then exacted revenge for their defeat to Australia in the Oceania Rugby U20 Championship with a 55-24 victory over the young Wallabies in the fifth-place final. As is normal, New Zealand had a squad packed with talent, the stand-out players being centre Jordie Barrett, full back Shaun Stevenson, second-row Hamish Dalzell and centre Peter Umaga-Jensen.

Wales claimed the place below Australia after defeating Scotland 42-19 in the seventh-place play-off, but for the young Welshmen this was a disappointing tournament, having come into the championship as U20 Six Nations Grand Slam winners. But at least the Welsh fly-half production line has not been idle, as the emergence of Dan Jones and Jarrod Evans confirmed.

Scotland, with two Edinburgh and two Glasgow professional players in their squad and having beaten England in the Six Nations, had been hoping to finish higher than their best ever eighth position achieved in 2015. In their opening match the Scots looked poised to realise their objective after causing a seeding upset with a first ever win over Australia, but the cost was tournament-ending injuries to two key backs, and the beginning of what would be a high injury toll extending to ten over the championship.

The reality is that there is little depth at this level in Scottish rugby and the judgment has to be that yet again a mainly amateur side punched above their weight. For Scotland the Under 20 championship is about developing players, and encouragingly Scotland may have found a future international fly half in the shape of Adam Hastings, son of Gavin.

Elsewhere, the tournament was a disaster for France, who finished ninth, one place above championship debutants Georgia. Italy avoided the drop and it was Japan, despite playing some hugely exciting rugby, who were relegated.

The World Rugby U20 Championship 2017 will be held in Georgia. It will be a hot tournament in many senses and doubtlessly less moist than in Manchester, but if it can match the sheer excitement and unpredictability of the 2016 event, then hold on to your (sun) hats.

Beyond the Pyrenees
the Advance of Spanish Rugby

by **CHRIS THAU**

'Nava, who captained Spain at the World Rugby Nations Cup in Romania, believes that in order to succeed, the players must eliminate the small errors that affect their game'

T he fact that both Spanish Sevens teams, men and women, qualified for the Olympics is perhaps fortunate but not entirely accidental. It reflects the quality of the available talent in a country that could potentially become a powerhouse of Continental rugby. Next year the Spanish Rugby Federation (FER) celebrates 90 years since it commenced playing international rugby, yet despite its

ABOVE The Spain squad at the 2016 World Rugby Nations Cup tournament in Romania.

current sizeable powerbase of over 50,000 players and 200-plus clubs, Spain still hovers somewhere between the second and third tiers of the international game. The standard of the domestic game has been making hesitant progress, though it remains the Achilles' heel in the overall blueprint for success and elevated status. The causes are diverse in a heavily regionalised country that includes rugby strongholds of the likes of Catalonia, the Basque Country, Castile (Valladolid) and Madrid. An example of the inadequate standard of Spanish club rugby was offered by the brief foray into the European club game of the 2015 Spanish champions El Salvador, demolished 36-7 by the Italian club Viadana and 62-12 by Calvisano in the qualifiers for last year's European Rugby Challenge Cup.

The first rugby club in the country, Unió Esportiva Santboiana, was formed in 1921 in Sant Boi de Llobregat, a Barcelona suburb, by the 28-year-old Baudilio Aleu Torres, a veterinary surgeon, who had learned the game during his university days in Toulouse. The first photograph of the Santboiana team dates from 1921, but in 1922 they won the first tournament, played for the 'Royal Society of Horse Racing' Cup, which involved three other Barcelona clubs – the beginning of organised domestic rugby in Spain. The Catalan Rugby Federation was formed in 1922 in Barcelona, and the Spanish Federation the following year with Aleu Torres as president. Though there is evidence of rugby activity in Madrid before and after the Great War, the charted progress of the game in the Spanish capital starts in May 1923, when Biarritz Olympique took on Stadoceste Tarbais in a promotional game sponsored by the French Federation.

The match was played at the Metropolitan Stadium, in front of a large crowd, which included King Alfonso XIII of Spain and his wife Queen Victoria. It appears that the king was a great rugby fan, as his presence at Bordeaux's Stade du Parc Lescure for the 1924 French Championship final between Toulouse and Perpignan would indicate. It is not known if he watched Spain's first ever international match against France, whose team included the legendary Yves du Manoir, in Madrid in 1927, but he was definitely in the stand of Barcelona's newly built Montjuic Stadium for the third Spanish international, against Italy in 1929. In the past year, the royal family have rekindled their relationship with rugby, with King Felipe VI attending the eighty-third final of the Copa del Rey, contested by the El Salvador and Entrepinares clubs in front of a record domestic crowd of more than 26,000 in Valladolid.

The tug of war between the two leading rugby centres of Madrid and Barcelona endured during the 1920s and 1930s, and was initially reflected in the selection policy of the national team. No Catalans represented Spain in that first Test against France in 1927, and no Madrid players appeared in the Spanish team that beat Italy 9-0 in 1929; the Madrid-based teams were captained by Francisco Martínez Larrañaga and the Catalans skippered by Joaquín Fontanella Castro. By the 1930s the Spanish had played against most Western European countries, including France, Germany and Portugal, and the centre of gravity of Spanish rugby had moved to Madrid, with Larrañaga elected FER president in 1933. In an act of defiance the Catalan Federation became one of the founding members of the Continental rugby body, Fédération Internationale de Rugby Amateur (FIRA), in 1934, but did not take part in its competitions, then the civil war that broke out in Spain in 1936 brought all rugby activity to a halt. The last international match before the war was against Portugal in 1936, while Italy provided the opposition for the first match after the war in 1951. Spanish rugby continued to develop, and the national team, who kept producing outstanding players, narrowly failed to qualify for RWC 1991, with Gérard Murillo as coach. Despite Spanish rugby's largely amateur structure, Spain managed to qualify for RWC 1999, the first professional Rugby World Cup tournament, with former international centre Alfonso Feijoo, a Basque and the current president of the federation, as head coach and Alberto Malo, a Catalan from UE Santboiana, as captain.

At the time, the current head coach of Spain, Santiago Santos Muñoz, a former international hooker and captain, felt that an inadequate domestic structure prevented the progress of the

RIGHT An aerial duel during the Nations Cup encounter between Spain (in red) and an Argentina XV. The South Americans won the match 44-8.

FACING PAGE Spain v Italy in Barcelona 1929. This was Italy's first ever international match; Spain's third.

Spanish game. Santos, a PE teacher by trade, who won 45 caps for his country between 1980 and 1992, most of them as captain 1984-92, has developed his coaching philosophy and practice in Spain, England and New Zealand. To hone his coaching skills, he travelled to London, where he spent six years playing amateur rugby for the Wasps 2nds and 3rds, and to Christchurch, where he worked with the late Laurie O'Reilly at the university and with Wayne Smith, at the time development officer of the Canterbury Union. 'I spent a whole season in New Zealand, talking a lot to O'Reilly and shadowing Smith as he coached the Canterbury 2nd XV and all the age-group sections. I was like a sponge; absorbing everything they did and said. I was trying to understand why Spanish players could not maintain playing quality rugby for more than two to three minutes at a time. I realised that consistency has a lot to do with intensity in training. If you want to perform you have to train at 100 per cent intensity and 100 per cent concentration all the time, also maintaining a high skill standard. There is no other option. It is a mental skill that needs acquiring and developing, as we are not born with it. You play the way you train, this is what they say. By then I had studied Villepreux's general movement theory and I was trying to combine it with some traditional New Zealand coaching. So culturally, I am a kind of melting pot of rugby cultures: I learnt a lot from my former Spain coach Gérard Murillo, from my New Zealand teachers Wayne Smith and Laurie O'Reilly, from Pierre Villepreux and from my former Youth coach Morgan Thomas, a Welshman who coached Spain Under 19 and the seniors for a short while.'

During an earlier tour, the 1984 Jaguars to South Africa, Santos recognised the role played by regional competition in talent identification and selection. 'So, on my return I wrote a proposal to the Spanish Union to start a regional competition in Spain, similar to South Africa and New Zealand,' he said. 'There was nothing too clever! I was not trying to reinvent the wheel. I said, just look at what other nations are doing. We do not want revolution; evolution is the way forward. Well, I failed. I realised then how difficult it is to change the mentality and the culture of Spanish rugby. Even now, the key issue that holds us back is the low standard of teaching at grass-root level. There is an old saying in Spanish that could apply to what happens: *¡Es como sembrar en el desierto!* [It is like planting seeds in the desert!] Unlikely to grow!'

This is why Santos, who commenced coaching as soon as his playing days came to an end, travels around following Spain age-group selections, as if his life depends on it. And maybe it does indeed, as he passionately believes that talent identification in rugby is a life-long process that starts very early. While working hard with his senior squad, he followed both the Under 18s and Under 19s to the European Championship tournaments in 2015, and then this year he travelled to Zimbabwe to encourage his right-hand men and assistant coaches Miguel Velasco and Pierre Montlaur, who are in charge of Spain Under 20, who surprised the world and themselves by narrowly losing the World Rugby U20 Trophy final 38-32 to the blockbusting Samoa.

For a short while Santos was assistant national coach and director of coaching of FER, then he took over as coach of the La Moraleja club, where he spent eight years taking them from the fourth division to the first division. It was after La Moraleja that he went to London before recommencing his coaching career. As an assistant coach he helped Cisneros achieve promotion to the Spanish first division and after a brief stint as an assistant national team coach, he was appointed national selector and head coach of Spain at the beginning of the 2013-14 season, the beginning of a new era in Spanish rugby.

His aim is to develop a joint team approach, 'a team that thinks collectively'. 'Getting 15 individuals to subscribe to the same playing approach and tactical thinking is my aim,' he said.

'I want the players to instinctively react as a group to the changing tactical contexts and my role is giving them the tools to achieve that. I do not want to create robots. It is the decision-making process that is crucial to all that and individuality plays a big role in this. It is a flexible approach in which the ball carrier is the decision maker and everyone else around him must instinctively react to what he is doing.

'Rugby is growing fast in Spain. The numbers have doubled in the last ten years and the game is getting bigger and stronger. Spain is a big country, with over 45 million people. The Spanish people are discovering the values of rugby and the game is on the brink of a major advance. The game is increasingly visible in the media and on TV, and the number of spectators is up. The results of our national team are ever more important. Although perhaps the rate of the team's success does not match the expectations, the playing style is more and more important. That can only be achieved by players who enjoy what they are doing. This is crucial to the success of the project. It is all in the head – this is why a lot of preparation goes into what we do off the field. At the same time having fun in training makes it easier.'

Santos has surrounded himself with a group of rugby workaholics who subscribe to his philosophy and practice. His assistant coaches Velasco and Montlaur work with both the senior squad and the highly successful Under 20s; Mar Alvarez is the fitness and conditioning coach, probably the only woman at this level in international rugby, with José Manuel Pérez as manager and former French full back Jean-Michel Aguirre as ambassador and occasional team manager. 'What is more important is that the players are buying into Santos' philosophy. It is the players who push things forward and I believe the results will start to materialise soon,' Aguirre pointed out.

Jaime Nava, a former centre-threequarter who turned into a dynamic and blockbusting No. 8, is Santos' agent on the field of play. Nava, who captained Spain at the World Rugby Nations Cup in Romania, believes that in order to succeed, the players must eliminate the small errors that affect their game. 'Every single player in this team believes in the project. There are weaknesses in our game, which we need to iron out, if we want to move forward. We play well for a period of time, then we make an error. We lose concentration for a short while and all the good work goes down the drain. It is all about small details that hold us back. RWC 2019 is a reasonable target for us, 20 years since Spain [last] played in the RWC. But to qualify, we must move the next step up, in terms of concentration and intensity. That should help us to make the difference.'

Fiji First
the HSBC WR Sevens
Series
by PAUL BOLTON

'I can't go to the supermarket without getting mobbed. If I am out in the city, in Suva, I will probably get 200-300 photographs a day. It is very surreal'

It was a Sevens season to forget for England, but for one Englishman the 2015-16 HSBC World Series represented a personal success story. Ben Ryan, who coached the England Sevens team from 2007 to 2013, guided Fiji to back-to-back titles for the first time, clinching the championship, with delicious irony, at Twickenham when Fiji reached the quarter-finals of the last tournament of an expanded series.

ABOVE Fiji's Jasa Veremalua, DHL Impact Player for the series, touches down against England in the Cup final in Dubai.

Ryan played for Loughborough University, Cambridge University, Nottingham and West Hartlepool and cut his coaching teeth as director of rugby with Newbury when they were in what is now the RFU Championship. He impressed as an innovative and imaginative coach and took his first steps on the international coaching ladder as assistant coach of England Counties in 2005 and head coach of the side two years later. He succeeded Mike Friday as national Sevens coach and during his time guided England to the RWC Sevens final in 2013 – their best placing in 20 years – and 28 semi-finals or better in 56 World Series tournaments.

But, worn down by the internal machinations of the RFU's desire to homogenise their coaching structure, Ryan resigned in 2013. He was not out of work for long. Fiji recognised Ryan's talents and put him in charge of their Sevens set-up in September of the same year. Although Ryan had to work on a shoestring budget and had to dip into his own pocket to pay for petrol for the team bus during his first six months in charge, the financial situation improved and the high profile of Sevens rugby in Fiji has given him cult status in the country.

'I can't go to the supermarket without getting mobbed,' Ryan told *The Daily Telegraph*. 'If I am out in the city, in Suva, I will probably get 200-300 photographs a day. It is very surreal. The closest thing I can compare it to is being manager of the Brazil football team. Everyone knows who you are. I mean everyone, so I get mobbed like I am Brad Pitt whenever I step out of the house.'

Despite his success with Fiji Ryan can still walk around London, his home city, in happy anonymity as Sevens has been the poor relation to the 15-a-side game in England, the situation not being helped by the national side finishing a poor eighth in the 2015-16 series. England, coached by Simon Amor who succeeded Ryan three years ago, began the series well, finishing as runners-up to Fiji in the Cup competition in the series opener in Dubai in December. But they failed to make the final of the top-tier competition again, with a 19-0 victory over the United States in the Plate final in Hong Kong proving the highlight of a depressing campaign. There was one significant individual contribution from England, with James Rodwell, the former Moseley back-row forward, setting a new HSBC World Series record of consecutive tournament appearances in Singapore. That was Rodwell's sixty-ninth tournament in a row, one more than South Africa's Frankie Horne.

Wales also disappointed, trailing in twelfth although they won the Bowl competition in both Las Vegas and Twickenham and the Shield in Sydney where they beat Russia in the final. Scotland provided the highlight for the three Home Nations by beating South Africa 27-26 at Twickenham to win a Cup title for the first time, having earlier won the Bowl three times: in Cape Town, where they beat England 19-0 in the final; Singapore, with a 14-10 win over the United States; and Paris, where England were vanquished 28-10.

By the time Fiji reached Twickenham, Ryan's side knew that they needed only to reach the last eight and collect eight points to defend their crown. Despite the inclusion of former Australia rugby league star Jarryd Hayne, Fiji were beaten by England in their pool opener, but wins over Wales and Australia gave them the title, ten points ahead of South Africa.

Fiji's successful campaign included Cup wins in Dubai, Las Vegas and Hong Kong, runners-up places in Singapore and Paris and a Plate win in Cape Town. Jasa Veremalua's contribution to Fiji's success was recognised with the DHL Impact Player award for racking up some impressive statistics which included 69 offloads, 135 carries, 116 tackles and 40 breaks.

Kenya's progress as a Sevens-playing nation continued with an historic first Cup win in Singapore where they beat Fiji 30-7 in the final. That victory helped Kenya to finish seventh in the standings, six points clear of England. Collins Injera scored two tries in the Singapore final and later became the leading try scorer in Sevens World Series history when he scored four on the opening day at Twickenham to break the previous record of 230 set by Santiago Gómez Cora of Argentina.

Seabelo Senatla of South Africa was the leading try scorer of 2015-16 with 66, with Madison Hughes of the United States contributing 331 points, including 108 conversions. In all 2622 tries and 16,469 points were scored across the ten tournaments, which included a new stop-off in Vancouver and the return of the Singapore and France Sevens in place of tournaments previously staged in Japan and Scotland. The Australia leg moved from the Gold Coast to Sydney and the South Africa Sevens to Cape Town from Port Elizabeth.

Having attracted 715,000 spectators across the globe, the HSBC World Rugby Sevens Series will visit the same cities again in 2016-17. As the schedule was announced, Bill Beaumont, the new chairman of World Rugby, said, 'We welcomed five new locations to the series in 2015-16 and each were tremendous additions and we now look ahead to an exciting 2016-17 HSBC World Rugby Sevens Series that will springboard the sport into a new Olympic Games cycle, reaching and inspiring new audiences worldwide.'

FACING PAGE James Rodwell of England in action against Portugal during the Singapore leg of the series, his record-breaking sixty-ninth consecutive tournament.

BELOW Scott Riddell and Dougie Fife celebrate the latter's winning try against South Africa at Twickenham that brought Scotland their first Cup title.

Fortune favours the brave

And the doggedly determined

There's ambition in all of us. At HSBC we're
here to support you in any way we can.

Proud supporter of the Wooden Spoon

HSBC

Issued by HSBC Holdings plc.

Olympic Sevens Women: Australia's Historic Gold
by SARA ORCHARD

'Favourites from the start, Australia lived up to their billing, going unbeaten throughout. Back home their triumph was celebrated with a $1 stamp showing the victorious side'

The passion and skill on display by the women rugby Sevens players at Rio 2016 won over the hearts and minds of any doubters as the sport quickly became an Olympic fans' favourite. The honour of winning the first Olympic rugby gold medal since 1924 went to Australia's women. Favourites from the start, they lived up to their billing, going unbeaten throughout. Back home their triumph was celebrated with a $1 stamp showing the victorious side with their medals. Following the conclusion of the women's Olympic tournament, World Rugby chairman Bill Beaumont declared, 'We have seen women's rugby launched on a truly global stage. Stars have been born; unforgettable moments created and fans entertained. Congratulations to our gold medallists Australia, but to all our women Olympians, thank you, you have made your families, nations and rugby proud. You have made history.'

ABOVE New Zealand's Kelly Anne Brazier cannot stop Evania Pelite putting Australia into a lead that they never again relinquished in the gold medal match in Rio.

The impact of the tournament on the popularity and professionalism of women's rugby is expected to be significant and global. The benefits are expected to be felt in both Sevens and 15-a-side rugby as barriers continue to be broken down between the men's and women's games.

The Rio event was contested by 12 nations split into three pools, with the seedings determined by the combined points tally from the results of the 2014-15 and 2015-16 World Series. Each team played the three other countries in their pool on a round-robin basis, with the top two sides in each pool, along with the two best third-placed teams, qualifying for the quarter-finals. Those outside this top eight continued playing for places nine to 12, while the losing quarter-finalists went on to contest places five to eight.

The first match to grace the turf at the Deodoro Stadium was France against Spain. The honour of the first try to be touched down went to France's Camille Grassineau as the French came through to win 24-7. During the pool stage there was only one upset, when seventh-seeded Fiji beat sixth seeds USA, although the odd eyebrow was raised when eventual champions Australia drew their final pool match with the USA 12-12. The most eagerly anticipated pool game saw third seeds Canada lose 22-0 to Great Britain who were ranked fourth. This result left the Great Britain team at the top of the pool, although the two sides would meet again later in the competition.

The quarter-finals went according to seedings, although New Zealand's Black Ferns beat the USA just 5-0. This set up a semi-final between New Zealand and Great Britain after the latter beat Fiji 26-7. The other quarter-finals would see Australia thump Spain 24-0 and Canada overcome France 15-5.

BELOW Kelly Russell scores her side's fourth first-half try as Canada take the bronze medal match away from Great Britain.

On Monday 8 August the final matches of the women's Sevens were played out in front of an excited Deodoro crowd who had quickly grown to love the Olympics' newest sporting offering. The first semi-final was between Canada and Australia, and the star of the match was the Aussies' Emilee Cherry. The 2014 IRB Women's Sevens Player of the

Year scored twice in the first half to put her side 12-0 up at the break. Chloe Dalton added a third score in the second half and despite a last-ditch Canadian effort by Charity Williams the Australians were heading into the gold medal match, with the final scoreline 17-5.

The second semi saw second seeds New Zealand face Great Britain. Despite a promising opening spell by Team GB, the Black Ferns went ahead through Portia Woodman. The former netball player comes from a family of All Blacks, with both her father Kawhena and uncle Fred having donned the jersey. After GB had taken a 7-5 lead through Alice Richardson's converted score, New Zealand tries rained down. In a minute of high drama Team GB saw both Katy Mclean and Amy Wilson Hardy sent to the sin-bin. The loss of both players simultaneously proved too much for the British side. Ruby Tui and Huriana Manuel added their names to the scoresheet for New Zealand as Woodman touched down twice more for the 25-7 win and the chance to play Australia in the gold medal match.

It left Great Britain and Canada in the battle for bronze, a repeat of their pool clash which the Brits had won so convincingly. The story was not to be repeated. Karen Paquin opened the Canadian scoring account, only for 2014 World Cup winner Danielle Waterman to briefly reduce the scoreline to just two points. It didn't last long as Ghislaine Landry crossed the whitewash for a converted try to give her country a 14-5 lead. Then the curse of the sin-bin struck the Brits again as captain Emily Scarratt saw yellow for a deliberate knock-on and Canada took off.

Ruthless in their response to Great Britain's numerical disadvantage, by half-time the Canadians had two more tries through Bianca Farella and Kelly Russell to give them a 26-5 lead. Wales's Jasmine Joyce pulled back a score for GB, but Landry crossed once more for Canada to secure the 33-10 win and the Olympic bronze medal.

Canada's Ashley Steacy had overcome knee surgery in double quick time to win selection for Rio and couldn't have been prouder of her team's efforts. 'It's amazing. We were obviously going for gold and Australia played a really great game against us [in the semi-final]. What defines you is how you bounce back from that and I think we really proved it out there, we wanted it.'

As the Canadians celebrated, there was tearful despair for Great Britain who would leave Rio empty-handed. Despite the bitter disappointment, captain Emily Scarratt was able to find some solace in the occasion. 'This has been a phenomenal experience, bringing rugby to the Olympic world stage. It has been amazing. And if we have inspired a couple of people back home, we are doing a decent job. We are just sorry we could not bring home a medal.'

The gold medal match was contested by two old friends from across the ditch, Australia and New Zealand. Perhaps the writing had been on the wall with Australia winning their last four encounters. Arguably both teams saved their best rugby for the final, opening with bruising defensive efforts, eventually broken by the Black Ferns' Kayla McAlister, who scored in the corner. The Australians rallied and eventually Emma Tonegato got on the scoresheet.

The decisive moment in the final saw New Zealand's Woodman sent to the sin-bin for a deliberate knock-on. She would later rue her years as a netball player for the mistake. Evania Pelite's try for Australia put them 10-5 ahead and was followed quickly by another from Ellia Green. By the time Charlotte Caslick took a quick tap penalty to score, the match was out of reach for New Zealand. A last-ditch try by Portia Woodman brought the score to 24-17, but the Australians were able to celebrate their gold medal before the Kiwis had even kicked the conversion. Australia were Olympic champions, New Zealand would have to settle for the silver medal.

The Black Ferns' Sarah Goss was honest as she summed up her emotions at the final whistle. 'To be honest, pretty gutted. We came out here to win a gold medal and we are bringing back a silver. But silver's still good in New Zealand's eyes and we hope we have done them proud.'

With tears streaming down the faces of the devastated Black Ferns, they still had the character and bravery to perform the haka for the New Zealand fans who had come to Rio to support them. As for Australia, their delight as Olympic champions was described by try scorer Ellia Green. 'I have this gold medal around my neck. But during the game I didn't even think of it as the gold medal match. This is just another game. We had to empty the tank, and that's what the girls did.

'Our hearts and our parents, friends, families and supporters back home were right on our chest. We played for them and Australia.'

As Olympic debuts go, the women's rugby Sevens at Rio will surely pave the way for many more glorious Olympic days ahead.

Eastdil Secured

is proud to support

Wooden Spoon Rugby World

Men: Deodoro Is El Dorado

by IAN ROBERTSON

'In the whole history of the Olympic Games, Fiji had never, ever won a medal of any colour. Now in Rio, the Fijians were expected to fly back home clutching 12 gold medals'

H aving hosted the women's rugby competition, the newly built stadium at Deodoro on the outskirts of Rio de Janeiro was home to three further glorious days of Sevens rugby as the men took to the arena. It had been an excellent decision to feature Sevens when the International Olympic Committee voted to include rugby once again in Rio. Unlike the 15-a–side game, Sevens is very easy to follow. It is fast, direct, exciting, dramatic and bursting with non-stop action and fantastic ball-handling skills for the seven minutes each way of every tie.

ABOVE Thousands upon thousands of Fijians turn out to welcome their heroes home after their gold medal win in Rio.

Fiji were the top-ranked men's team going into the Olympics after the 2015-16 HSBC World Series of ten tournaments in a host of exotic locations: Dubai, Cape Town, Wellington, Sydney, Las Vegas, Vancouver, Hong Kong, Singapore, Paris and London. Fiji appeared in five Cup finals and won three and went to Rio as the favourites. After all, the Fijians do have certain advantages over other teams. They are bigger, heavier, stronger, faster and better ball players. Nevertheless it is hard to imagine the enormous pressure on the 12-man Fijian squad and also on their English coach, Ben Ryan. In the whole history of the Olympic Games, Fiji had never, ever won a medal of any colour. Now in Rio, in August 2016, the Fijians were expected to fly back home clutching 12 gold medals.

The phenomenal weight of expectation must have been overwhelming and claustrophobic. The population of Fiji is about 880,000. The three biggest sports in Fiji are rugby followed by rugby and then rugby. It is the ultimate pinnacle of every male Fijian's ambition to play international rugby for Fiji. The game is an obsession and a passion. It is for them the equivalent of climbing to the top of Everest. It is one thing to be favourites for a tournament – it is another thing to win it. Could 100 years of history be cast aside to allow one wonderful South Sea island to enjoy and savour the greatest day in their sporting history? Watching the Sevens from the main grandstand was Fiji's prime minister – Frank Bainimarama. I met him each day as Fiji won each of their pool matches, beating Brazil 40-12, Argentina 21-14 and the USA 24-19.

The knockout stages are much harder, but Fiji remained cool and confident, meeting and beating third seeds New Zealand in the first quarter-final, the score 12-7. That was rather close, but back home, with the whole population clustered around television sets and radios in every town and village in Fiji, a collective sigh of relief kept the dream alive. Japan, seeded tenth, then beat eighth seeds France, also 12-7, and in the bottom half of the draw, Great Britain, ranked fourth, beat seventh seeds Argentina 5-0 and South Africa, seeded second, beat fifth seeds Australia 22-5.

The quarter-final between Great Britain and Argentina was a really remarkable match. I watched it with the renowned Sevens expert Rob Vickerman who played nine years in the England Sevens team – the last three years as captain before retiring in 2013. He knows everything about Sevens. At half-time the score was 0-0. I asked what happened if it stayed 0-0 at full time. 'Impossible,' he replied. In the 170 tournaments of the HSBC World Series no game had ever ended 0-0 at full time. This quarter-final did. It was a little piece of history. It was still 0-0 in the fifth minute of extra time sudden death (first team to score wins). It was at that point that Dan Bibby sprinted through a gap to score the try which took Great Britain through to the semi-finals, where they beat South Africa 7-5. In the other semi-final Fiji beat Japan 20-5. Everything had fallen into place perfectly. Fiji – the people's favourite – against Great Britain – the British people's favourite.

It is important and significant to point out that Team GB had performed superbly on their way to the final. They showed great form to beat New Zealand, Kenya and Japan in Pool C: played 3, won 3. They then beat Argentina and arguably they surpassed expectations in beating South Africa in the semi-finals. The Great Britain Sevens team did Britain proud and they deserve to be praised to the hilt for reaching the Olympic final and winning silver medals. I emphasise this because the final was one-sided. No Sevens team in the world could have stopped Fiji in Deodoro at 7pm on 11 August 2016. The Fijians were comprehensively sublime, totally brilliant, combining truly exceptional and quite outrageous skills with a complete understanding of the art of Sevens.

It was a spellbinding masterclass. Five tries in the first half – the scorers were Kolinisau (57 seconds), Tuwai (3 minutes 25 seconds), Veremalua (6 minutes 59 seconds), Nakarawa (8 minutes), Ravouvou (9 minutes 59 seconds). The final is ten minutes each way. At half-time Fiji led 29-0. In the second half, Fiji got two more tries through Tuisova and Mata. Also in the second half, Great Britain – bloodied but unbowed – had the satisfaction/consolation of Dan Norton scoring their only try of the match.

Up until this Olympic final, the greatest day in Fijian rugby took place in the summer of 1977 when Fiji beat the British & Irish Lions 25-21 in Suva as the Lions were on their way home from their tour of New Zealand. That posed a difficult question for their prime minister in Rio – which was the greatest ever day for Fiji? Beating the Lions in 1977? Or winning Olympic gold in 2016? His answer was perfect. The win over the Lions in 1977 was the best ever day for Fiji in 15-a-side rugby; 2016 in Rio was the best ever day for Fijian Sevens.

Roll on Japan in 2020. As for Rio 2016, a great effort by Great Britain to win silver. And congratulations to Fiji, the consummate heroes of the Sevens tournament. Deodoro for them was all about gold. El Dorado is about gold. And cometh the hour, Japan will be all about gold.

Footnote
There is one nice link between 1977 and 2016. In 1977, the Fijian legend Samisoni Viriviri was one of the stars of the Fijian team to beat the Lions. In 2016, his grandson, also Samisoni Viriviri, was one of Fiji's Sevens stars.

FACING PAGE, TOP Great Britain's Dan Bibby steps inside the Argentine defence to score the sudden-death try that took Team GB through to a semi-final against second seeds South Africa.

LEFT Osea Kolinisau, the Fiji skipper, opens his side's account in the first minute of the gold medal match as the South Sea islanders power past Great Britain to become Olympic champions.

INSPIRING COMMUNITIES & CHANGING LIVES
THROUGH THE POWER OF SPORT

The Saracens Sport Foundation uses sport to engage some of the most disadvantaged and challenging young people in our community. By using sport as the vehicle to address social issues we aim to create better life chances for those involved.

For more information on how you can get involved changing lives through sport visit us att **www.saracens.com/foundatio**

Allianz Park, Greenlands Lane, Hendon, London, NW4 1RL | 0203 675 7243 registered charity number: 1079316

WWW.SARACENS.COM/FOUNDATION

🐦 @saracenssportfo   f SaracensSportFoundation

Summer Tours 2016
England in Australia

by **MICK CLEARY**

'Third Test, same outcome, albeit with the astonishing scoreline of Australia 40 England 44 – another record mark. It was a seminal performance by England'

Many have travelled from these parts to Australia for a spot of hard labour and self-correction. And even if these days it is a voluntary and brief exile, it has tended to be a painful experience for our rugby teams. With a return of only three wins from 17 Test matches, England have tended to travel in hope rather than any expectation.

Few might have imagined, then, that it would be Eddie Jones's touring party dishing out all the lessons. True, England were Grand Slam champions of Europe. True, they had an Australian at the helm, with another son of those distant shores, Glen Ella, hired to do a number for this trip alone. England were unbeaten under

ABOVE Man of the match James Haskell of England bursts from a maul and charges upfield to set up a try for Marland Yarde in the first Test in Brisbane.

Jones, and headed off to Heathrow on a Tuesday morning in June also boosted by a hearty 27-13 win over Wales two days earlier. And that by an England side shorn of ten players from Exeter and Saracens involved in the Aviva Premiership final. Yes, England were in their pomp. But who really would have bet on a clean sweep against a Wallaby side that had brushed them aside so easily in that epoch-defining World Cup game only eight months earlier? There had been a changing of the guard at the top of English rugby, with Jones being brought in to replace Stuart Lancaster, but the playing personnel were largely the same.

Well, they appeared so. The naked eye may not have been able to discern much difference, apart, admittedly, from the highly influential second-row pairing of George Kruis and Maro Itoje. But internally England were made of different stuff. That much had been in evidence during the 2016 Six Nations Championship. Eddie had got inside their heads. And it worked.

The tour squad itself did not throw up too many surprises, the one notable exception being the omission of Chris Ashton. 'It wasn't a tough [selection] call to make, it was an easy call to make,' said Jones. 'We want players who are going to grow. Chris has scored a lot of tries but there is a part of the game where you don't have the ball. I pick the side on what I need for the team. I don't pick it on popular demands. One of the best pieces of advice I ever got was that if you listen to the fans you'll end up in the grandstand with them.'

BELOW Prelude to pandemonium. Jamie George kicks upfield 75 minutes into the second Test in Melbourne and sets off in pursuit ... Seconds later Owen Farrell (**FACING PAGE**) pounces on the bouncing ball to score under the posts. England cannot be caught and have won their first series in Australia.

That no-nonsense approach, stripped of all sentimentality, is what has always marked out Jones. It has become a characteristic of his teams, too. It is about winning, not about being popular.

If there was one person who knew all about that tough-guy streak in Jones, it was his old Randwick mucker, Wallaby coach Michael Cheika. He would not be taking anything for granted, all the more so given that he was without several of those World Cup front-liners, such as France-based Matt Giteau and Adam Ashley-Cooper, or injured stars such as Kurtley Beale. Even so, the Wallabies had a decent pack of forwards at their disposal, including their all-star back-row trio of Scott Fardy, David Pocock and Michael Hooper as well as the X-factor talent of Israel Folau at the rear. Australia would not be giving way lightly.

And so it proved, but give way they did, losing the first Test at the Suncorp Stadium in Brisbane, 39-28, a record score for England. Jones showed his ruthlessness again when substituting Luther Burrell after just 29 minutes, at which point Australia were two tries to the good from Hooper and Folau and looking threatening at every turn. The Northampton centre, a late tour call-up for the injured Manu Tuilagi, had gone straight into the Test side at the expense of George Ford who was dropped to the bench, with Owen Farrell starting at No. 10. England's defence was skewed and Jones made an immediate call when he realised what was happening. It was bold and decisive, England regrouping and weathering the storm before breaking out to score a first-half try by Jonathan Joseph.

Even though they appeared under the cosh, it was in fact Australia who were giving away penalties, allowing England easy points. Farrell, as was to be case throughout the series, was not of a mind to turn down such gifts. Six penalties (and three conversions) went over that night, England finishing by far the stronger, another theme that was to be repeated throughout the tour, tries from Marland Yarde and Jack Nowell, set against further Wallaby tries from Hooper and Tevita Kuridrani, seeing them to their landmark win. Flanker James Haskell was named man of the match with a fierce and unrelenting performance, typifying his team's desire in making 18 tackles. The Burrell-Ford substitution paid dividends, with the Bath fly half having a hand in two of England's three tries.

'It gave us more variety to our game,' said Jones. 'We had to make a decision for the interests of the team and that was one I had to make. We just needed to change the game. There are just times you do things through a gut feeling. If you change the game, you change personnel.'

There was to be no wallowing in the moment for England. Jones's mind was already focused on the second Test. 'We have made history today but it is not good enough for us,' said Jones. 'We need to make sure we have good focus. The Australians will come at us left, right and centre.'

England were back on the training ground in Melbourne within 36 hours of the final whistle sounding at Suncorp, with little sign of any let-up in intensity as they went through their vigorous paces in the well-appointed surroundings of Scotch College. There was no reason to make substantial changes, Ford resuming in the No. 10 shirt and Farrell continuing at inside centre. Once again, Jones had hit the key note, warning that Australia would be wounded and intent on coming at England.

And so they did. Again and again, wave after wave. But England held firm. It was a Rorke's Drift effort, resistance against all odds. England made 169 clean tackles as opposed to 49 by Australia, with some statisticians figuring that the England total was nearer 220, taking into account all those half-scragged efforts, all of which contributed. Jones termed it 'rope-a-dope', referencing the famous 1974 bout between Muhammad Ali and George Foreman, noting the manner in which England absorbed all that Australia could throw at them before hitting back at the end with a breakaway try from Owen Farrell who finished with another impressive haul of points, 18. Dylan Hartley scored England's other try in the 19th minute on the day that he became his country's most capped hooker. His opposite number, Stephen Moore, scored a similar drive-over try for the Wallabies, but they looked a worn-down, well-beaten side by the end of the series-clinching 23-7 England win.

RIGHT No stopping him from there. No. 8 Billy Vunipola flies off the back of the scrum close to the Australia line and batters down the Wallaby defence to score England's third try in Sydney.

Defence coach Paul Gustard had got his men in the right no-surrender mood by reading them a poem – *The Guy in The Glass* by Dale Wimbrow. 'I told the players that I had had lots of opportunities in life, off the field, on the field, and I wasted most of them,' recounted Gustard. 'During my career I would look at other people for the blame, I thought I trained and worked hard, but I didn't. I told them that this was their opportunity to make history, to do something different, to be special, and if they were to look at themselves at the end of the day, could they say that they had emptied themselves? I think today they did.'

Once again, Jones only had thoughts for what lay ahead, not for what had just happened. 'We want to be the best team in the world and we want to win the series 3-0,' said Jones. 'If the All Blacks were in this situation now, what would they be thinking? They'd be thinking 3-0.'

Once again, he hit the mark. Third Test, same outcome, albeit with the astonishing scoreline of Australia 40 England 44 – another record mark. It was a seminal performance by England, with yet another radical intervention by Jones who did as he had done with Burrell when hauling off rookie Northampton flanker Teimana Harrison after barely half an hour of play, realising that he needed to beef up the forward play. On came Courtney Lawes, back went Maro Itoje, and the intensity lifted several notches. Harrison had come in for the injured (toe) James Haskell. That Jones needed to make such a switch early in the game illustrates just how influential Haskell's power and abrasiveness had been.

Play ebbed and flowed, Dan Cole scored, Bernard Foley got one back for the Wallabies, then another came through wing Dane Haylett-Petty. Mike Brown got England back on track and all the time the boot of Farrell kept swinging. Even though England were eventually outscored by five tries to four – Billy Vunipola and Jamie George getting the other scores to tries from Hooper, Folau and Taqele Naiyaravoro – there was no doubt as to who were the more rounded side. Farrell finished with 24 points.

It was 'solar-system class' goal-kicking according to Jones. It was the first time the Wallabies had been whitewashed at home since South Africa did so in 1971.

Classy. Very classy. Even the All Blacks would have sat up and taken notice.

Scotland in Japan

by ALAN LORIMER

'As for the experience of touring to Japan, it could turn out to be a smart move for Scotland by giving the country's players a flavour of what to expect during the global event'

To paraphrase Evelyn Waugh's classification of schools and apply it to rugby, there are memorable tours, there are less memorable tours and there are ... tours. Scotland's 2016 summer tour to Japan undoubtedly slipped into the latter category.

The record books will show a 2-0 series win for Scotland over the Brave Blossoms, but the manner of victory and notably the lack of a Scottish try in the second Test left many observers wondering just what was actually gained from the tour.

One way to justify the winning-at-all-costs approach was the effect on Scotland's world ranking, which in turn could impact on the draw for the 2019 World Cup to be made in May 2017. As for the experience of touring to Japan, it could turn out to be a smart move for Scotland by giving the country's players a flavour of what to expect during the global event.

The World Cup, however, will be held at a later time of the year, in the period 20 September to 2 November, when the climate will be less enervating than in June. What is a constant, though, is the claustrophobic atmosphere of Japan's clogged-up cities, which can have an overwhelming effect on players less used to high population and traffic densities.

Some have portrayed Scotland's tour to Japan as being somewhat second grade, for the reason that Scotland were not playing one of the southern-hemisphere giants. This is correct in the obvious sense but wrong in another. Japan, it will be remembered, caused ripples in the

---

LEFT Scotland's Jonny Gray beats fellow second-row Hitoshi Ono of Japan to line-out ball during the first Test.

FACING PAGE WP Nel crashes through Japan's defence including scrum half Kaito Shigeno to score in Toyota City.

2015 World Cup by defeating South Africa and, like the emblematic sun, they are a rising rugby nation, doubtlessly helped by their recent entry into Super Rugby. Moreover, Japan have form on home soil. Back in 1989 a Scotland XV lost 28-24 in Tokyo and as recently as 2013 Wales, with a similar strength side, went down 23-8 to the Blossoms.

Much of Japan's success in the very recent past, of course, has had very much to do with the influence of Eddie Jones. After Jones's departure to England, New Zealander Mark Hammett, who had been in charge of Japan's Super Rugby franchise, the Sunwolves, took over as interim national coach, keeping the hot seat warm until the arrival of the next appointee, Jamie Joseph.

With reputations at stake, Scotland coach Vern Cotter could not risk taking anything but a strong squad to Japan for the 2016 summer tour. In the event Cotter was frustrated by the pre-tour loss of fly half Finn Russell and centre Alex Dunbar, the two most notable players on his injury list. Also unavailable was centre Mark Bennett, who had opted to go down the route of Sevens rugby, and there was, too, the late withdrawal of Tim Visser.

Fly half Ruaridh Jackson and centre Matt Scott were brought into the squad and there was a call-up for the 22-year-old Edinburgh-born and Millfield-educated centre Huw Jones, who plays for the Stormers, the South African Super Rugby side, and who had been on the Murrayfield radar for some time. Jackson was named in a familiar-looking Scotland team for the first international at the Toyota Stadium in Toyota City on 18 June. A late change saw Stuart McInally replace hooker Ross Ford, who had failed a fitness test.

In humid, energy-sapping conditions Scotland attempted to play with urgency, but inaccuracy and a certain amount of rustiness resulted in the Scots achieving limited success in the face of a committed and quick-engaging Japan defence. In the circumstances Scotland had to look to the boot of Greig Laidlaw for their early points. Meanwhile, Japan's resolve to play fast, running rugby soon paid off when a quick tap penalty released wing Yasutaka Sasakura down the right. Scotland's defence closed in, but quickly recycled ball allowed fly half Yu Tamura to send Japan's skipper and hooker Shota Horie in under the posts, Tamura adding the conversion. Two penalties by Laidlaw and one by Tamura kept Japan in the lead with the scoreline at 10-9, but in the final five minutes of the first half the match turned on two Japanese misjudgments.

First the influential flanker Hendrik Tui was sent to the sin-bin after being penalised for side entry at the maul, following an earlier warning. Then just three minutes later, Tui was joined by a second Japanese offender, Rikiya Matsuda, the replacement full back having been shown the yellow card for slapping down the ball to prevent Stuart Hogg's likely scoring pass reaching Tommy Seymour, leaving referee Ben O'Keeffe with no option but to award a penalty try.

It was a devastating double blow for Japan, who now trailed Scotland 16-10. Scotland's two-man numerical advantage soon had its effect early in the second half when prop WP Nel scored from close range after wing Damien Hoyland had been stopped inches short. Laidlaw converted from the touch line before exchanging penalty goals with Tamura for an eventual 26-13 win.

It had not been an elegant victory but it was a win. 'We got the essential, which was a victory, and we created a number of opportunities. Another week together will help improve cohesion and help to get some of those opportunities to stick,' suggested Cotter, adding, 'They turned over a fair number of balls to us, which enabled us to get the pressure off.'

Victory had not been without its physical cost. Alasdair Dickinson lasted only minutes before retiring with a hamstring injury and a similar fate befell centre Duncan Taylor. Gordon Reid was called out as replacement for Dickinson.

If Cotter thought that time together on tour would indeed 'improve cohesion' then the second Test match on 25 June at Ajinomoto Stadium in Tokyo was to prove his prediction a tad optimistic. For this match Cotter made six changes to his starting team, the most significant being the inclusion of scrum half Henry Pyrgos, who took over from Laidlaw as captain.

FACING PAGE Scotland head coach Vern Cotter in conversation with replacement back-row John Hardie after the second Test.

BELOW Having replaced Henry Pyrgos after 50 minutes of the second Test, Greig Laidlaw slots one of his four penalties. Pyrgos had already kicked three.

In the event the 'freshening up' of the team produced a stodgy performance by Scotland in the second Test. Only one try was scored and it was Japan who took that honour, a length-of-the-field score begun from a line out in the Brave Blossoms' 22-metre area. No. 8 Amanaki Mafi did the damage with a powerful run down the right flank, before feeding fellow back-row Shoukei Kin, who put scrum half Kaito Shigeno away for the try of the series. Tamura, who landed three penalty goals in the match, added the conversion.

The try was no more than the Brave Blossoms deserved, a showpiece score hugely appreciated by the 34,000 spectators, and most evidently by the occupants of the royal box, Japan's emperor and empress. Japan's accurate passing and their pace in attack had tested Scotland's defence to near destruction and with more careful finishing the Brave Blossoms might have added further such scores.

Scotland never really threatened the Japan line and it was no surprise when they trailed 13-9 at the break, their points having come from three penalty kicks by an otherwise out-of-form Pyrgos. Cotter's reaction at the interval was to replace the front row and a little later both half backs, Laidlaw coming on for Pyrgos, and Huw Jones, earning his first Scotland cap, in place of Jackson. Horne moved to fly half and Jones was slotted in at centre.

It proved a game-changing set of substitutions. WP Nel's presence restored stability in the scrum, while Laidlaw exerted authority, drawing a hitherto absent synergy of effort from the Scotland team. Scotland's steadied scrum then began to achieve dominance in the set-piece and with Japan finding disfavour with referee Marius Mitrea at the breakdown points and scrums, Laidlaw slowly clawed back points with four penalty goals to steer his side to a 21-16 win.

'I'm happy with the way the team applied pressure and finally got the result. It could have gone the other way.' admitted Cotter, adding, 'We weathered a very difficult first half, they flew into us and lifted the intensity from last week. It took us a while to wear them down, but we are happy with the result.'

Rugby commentators talk about 'winning ugly' and certainly the video nasty of this second Test will confirm the accuracy of such a description. But it was a win and psychologically any results are important for Scotland. And it's maybe worth recalling that Scotland's last visit to Japan 27 years ago was followed by the Scots' 1990 Grand Slam triumph. How Cotter would love history to repeat itself.

Wales in New Zealand

by GRAHAM CLUTTON

'It was not all doom and gloom. However, if Wales are to close the gap on the leading nations in the world, they will need to find an extra gear, or two, when the going gets tough'

When Wales set sail for New Zealand, there were hopes and, of course, there were genuine fears. By the time they left the Land of the Long White Cloud, their hopes of a series win or even a one-off Test match victory over the world champions had long since been dashed. Sadly, in contrast, their fears had been realised. A 3-0 Test series whitewash and a chastening midweek defeat at the hands of the Chiefs had left Warren Gatland's squad to reflect on yet another summer of discontent. It is now 29 years since Wales defeated one of the southern-hemisphere super nations Down Under.

Of course, there were highlights. Rhys Patchell, Matthew Morgan, Ellis Jenkins and Aled Davies were all given international exposure, whilst two first-half performances of note – in Auckland and Wellington – had twice given rise to thoughts that maybe, in at least one Test, the All Blacks would falter and allow Wales that first Test match victory over them since 1953. It was not to be and by the time the side arrived in Dunedin, they were 2-0 down and facing up to the inevitability of another fruitless excursion (results-wise) Down Under. New Zealand, who won the first Test 39-21 and the second 36-22, helped themselves to a hatful of tries and ran out 46-6 winners. Then there was the humiliation of a 40-7 hammering at the hands of a weakened Chiefs side.

For Gatland, however, the tour was about more than four defeats, if only in terms of hardening the resolve of his players ahead of another tough season of international rugby. It answered questions, as tours always do. It highlighted the strengths and weaknesses of his side and provided greater knowledge of what is needed to close the gap on those at the sharp end of the international game.

'We will take lessons home with us and we must make sure we apply them when we next get together as a team,' he said after the defeat in Dunedin. 'We have got to learn from this experience and take it back to the regions. However, it's been a good experience for the players to learn from.

'Defence will be a big work-on for us and we have learnt a great deal about collision dominance at the breakdown and how they accelerate into the contact area. It creates quick ball on attack and puts pressure on your defence. That was the big difference and is something we need to apply. You can get away with it sometimes in the northern hemisphere because teams aren't so aggressive at the breakdown.'

Even without the likes of Dan Lydiate, Alex Cuthbert and Leigh Halfpenny, Wales harboured high hopes as they came up against a new-look All Blacks squad, who had seen the likes of Dan Carter, Ma'a Nonu and Richie McCaw step down after the World Cup final victory at Twickenham. Coach Steve Hansen had included six uncapped players in his 32-man party, two of whom – Ardie Savea and Seta Tamanivalu – started on the bench in the first Test at Eden Park.

For long periods of the game, Wales showed signs of genuine combativeness, in all departments. They competed well at the breakdown, showed control at half back and used their obvious strength out wide. They were genuine contenders. Still, for all the effort, sweat and toil, the world champions, who boasted 720 caps in a starting line-up led by No. 8 Kieran Read, pulled away to a 27th consecutive victory over Wales.

Despite leading after an hour, Wales shipped 21 points thereafter, with wing Waisake Naholo scoring his second and Read and Nathan Harris also crossing in the final quarter; Julian Savea had early on touched down for the other New Zealand try. No. 8 Taulupe Faletau, who was the stand-out player for Gatland's Wales, and scrum half Rhys Webb helped themselves to tries, but they could not mark Alun Wyn Jones's 100th appearance for his country with a first win over

LEFT All Blacks captain and No. 8 Kieran Read runs over Wales's Gareth Anscombe on his way to scoring in the first Test at Auckland's Eden Park.

the All Blacks on New Zealand soil. It was an all too familiar story for Wales. Gatland said: 'We all learned a lot from that game and will be better for it next week.

'We feel we get better the longer we are together. They get to experience a lot more games than us at that level of intensity and they are more familiar with it. We were blowing a bit and they just kept coming. But there were a lot of positives to take out of that game. There were some lovely breaks. I said we had to be brave and be bold and we did that.'

With the dust having settled on the Auckland Test, Wales's midweek team travelled to face the Chiefs in Gatland's home city of Hamilton. It was meant to be a celebration of the Kiwi's homecoming. Sadly, it was anything but as an understrength Chiefs ran amok, outscoring Wales by six tries to one in front of the British & Irish Lions coaching and management hierarchy.

Hansen had questioned why Wales had taken on the extra midweek fixture in the middle of a three-Test series and by the time the Chiefs had left Wales wondering what had struck them, many Welsh supporters felt the same way. In a dismal first half, the Chiefs built up a 21-0 lead. Wales had three chances to score tries and duly squandered all three. In contrast, the Chiefs scored three times, with a fourth controversially ruled out by the television match official. Wales dominated the second half, in terms of territory and possession, but managed only one try, from replacement hooker Kristian Dacey. 'We've learned a lot about ourselves this week and some of the players,' said Gatland. He certainly had.

The coach made only two changes for the second Test in Wellington – Rhys Patchell, who had flown out as a replacement, stepped in at full back, with Liam Williams moving on to the wing to replace George North, who was already back in Wales nursing a hamstring injury. Luke Charteris returned at lock.

Unfortunately, the game followed a similar pattern to the first as the All Blacks closed off the series with a crushing second-half display. Alun Wyn Jones's 38th-minute try tied the scores at 10-10 at the interval. However, inspired by replacement outside half Beauden Barrett, the All Blacks scored four second-half tries through Ben Smith, Barrett, Naholo and Ardie Savea. Liam Williams and Jonathan Davies scored for Wales in a late flurry, but it was too little too late. Another opportunity lost, another defeat over which to mull.

Disappointed with the final outcome, Gatland said: 'I was pretty proud of that performance. There were two or three key moments in the game and that's the difference.

'We are creating chances and the players are aware of a couple of things that in the same situation, they will do it a little bit different.

'New Zealand are clinical and those are the small margins that we need to be better at. They tried to increase the tempo and what I was proud of was that we were the ones who stayed in the game towards the end. I was certainly pleased with the last 20 minutes.'

Unfortunately, with the series lost, there was only pride to play for as the squad set off for Dunedin. Sadly, it was the All Blacks who finished strongly with Hansen's Class of 2016 stretching their winning run over Wales to 29 games in 63 years. The tourists fought as hard as they had in losing the first two Tests, but the All Blacks were smarter in defence and sharper in attack. The end result was inevitable as first-half tries by wing Ben Smith and centre George Moala were followed by Barrett's latest contribution. The outside half added a second try in a 26-point haul, with hooker Dane Coles and Israel Dagg also touching down.

The margin of victory was the fifth-largest for the All Blacks against Wales, the biggest a 55-3 win in 2003 when the tourists were coached by Hansen. Now a World Cup winner with his home country, Hansen made 12 changes for this game, five of them in the starting XV, and said the risks were worth the potential rewards. They certainly were. Not for Gatland. He said: 'In fairness to the All Blacks I thought they were outstanding. I thought the pace of their back three caused us some problems and some of their collision dominance was pretty good as well.'

So Wales left for home with three more Test match defeats on which to reflect and a great deal of hard work to consider ahead of the upcoming autumn series and the 2017 Six Nations Championship. It was not all doom and gloom, it never is. However, if Wales are to one day close the gap on the leading nations in the world, they will need to find an extra gear, or two, when the going gets tough. As for the All Blacks, well, nothing else needs to be said. Even without their back-row talisman and Carter and Nonu too, they were simply too strong and fully deserving of yet another whitewash against Wales.

Ireland in South Africa

by PETER O'REILLY

'Given the final outcome, this must go down as a golden opportunity blown by the tourists. Confidence had been stratospheric after Cape Town'

The first thing to be said about Ireland's Test series in South Africa is that it was great entertainment. The reason SANZAR requested these three-match tours is that 'best of three' makes more commercial and more competitive sense than 'best of two' and sure enough, this series was ultra-competitive: remarkably, a margin of just six points between the sides in Cape Town, Johannesburg and Port Elizabeth, with the outcome in the balance right until the very last play of the final game at the Nelson Mandela Bay Stadium, as Ireland battered away in vain at the Springboks' try line.

The South African Rugby Union (SARU) can only have been delighted with proceedings and with crowds of 40,000-plus at a delicate time in South African rugby, when new national coach Allister Coetzee needs to deliver success while at the same time meeting the demands of politicians, who insist that the demographics of the Boks reflect the demographics of the country in general.

Indeed, Coetzee and SARU must be counting their blessings as well as their earnings. Winning the series 2-1 was one hell of an escape. As a working reporter on the tour, one of my outstanding memories was

FACING PAGE Stuart Olding, in the Ireland side for the first time since 2014, is subdued by Elton Jantjies (10) and Faf de Klerk in Johannesburg.

BELOW Ireland full back Jared Payne latches on to Luke Marshall's grubber to touch down for Ireland after 11 minutes of the first Test.

the look of dread on the face of a SARU official sitting alongside me in the press box at half-time in the second Test: precisely midway through the series, Ireland led 19-3 with one Test already in the bag and the Ellis Park crowd were booing the Boks off the pitch.

Given the final outcome, this must go down as a golden opportunity blown by the tourists. Confidence had been stratospheric after Cape Town – not only a first ever Irish Test win on South African soil but one achieved in remarkable circumstances, with only 14 men on the pitch after CJ Stander was controversially red-carded in the 23rd minute for his challenge on Pat Lambie. Indeed Ireland had only 13 for the ten minutes that Robbie Henshaw was in the sin-bin before half-time.

The tourists brought that confidence with them to Johannesburg and once again shackled the rather shaken-looking Boks with the simple efficiency and determination of their play to build a 16-point lead by the break, which was still intact going into the final quarter.

But the record books won't necessarily go into that detail. Nor will they show that Ireland were the better team for eight of the 12 quarters played in the series. They will only show the final result: South Africa 2 Ireland 1. End of story.

But there are elements of the story that need to be taken into account, mitigating circumstances if you will. For starters, it was always asking a lot to expect that Ireland could finish the series at the same pace they started, given this was at the end of a ridiculously long season, especially for those players who had been involved in the World Cup the previous autumn. To put it into context, those players had turned up for pre-World Cup training on 29 June 2015 and their season ended when they flew out of Port Elizabeth on 27 June 2016. That's a 365-day season, a farcical situation in a sport which places such physical demands on its participants.

Naturally, not everyone made it through to the end. Coach Joe Schmidt had hoped to bring experienced leaders like Peter O'Mahony and Sean O'Brien to combat the über-physical Bok loosies but had to travel without them, and without Cian Healy. The last game of the domestic season, the Guinness PRO12 final, brought worse news for Schmidt: Johnny Sexton, Luke Fitzgerald, Rob and Dave Kearney, all casualties.

This meant call-ups for Craig Gilroy, Ian Madigan and the Connacht pair of Tiernan O'Halloran and Matt Healy, neither of whom were remotely familiar with the patterns and calls Schmidt had been implementing over the course of the season. O'Halloran would subsequently describe the

weird mix of emotions – half-wonder, half-fear – as he tried to acclimatise while also sweating out the effects of Connacht's celebrations in Galway.

Wisely, therefore, Schmidt talked less in the build-up about winning the series, more about the opportunity to build depth. He said he would give all 32 tourists some game time if possible and he was true to his word.

There was a cost to this inclusiveness. By picking a relatively weak bench for the second Test in Johannesburg, Schmidt may have kept everyone feeling involved but he also left himself vulnerable to the Boks' murderous final-quarter fightback, inspired by the arrival off the Boks' bench of Ruan Combrinck, Warren Whiteley and Pieter-Steph du Toit. Ireland couldn't offer anything like the same impact and this was the turning of the series.

BELOW Tadhg Furlong, on at tight-head for Mike Ross after 51 minutes of the third Test, is hauled down in spectacular style by Faf de Klerk.

But there was a bigger picture to be viewed, as Schmidt explained before the Test in Johannesburg. As far as he was concerned, the tour was about creating competition for places in every position, and thus aiming to avoid a repeat of the World Cup quarter-final against

Argentina, when Ireland paid a big price for being over-reliant on players like Sexton, O'Mahony, O'Brien, Paul O'Connell and Jared Payne. And in this regard, the tour was largely successful.

Coming into the tour, Schmidt's three danger spots were tight-head prop, scrum half and fly half. The team is still badly overdependent on Conor Murray but in the other two positions, the tour was enormously productive.

With Mike Ross now in his 37th year, it was imperative that Tadhg Furlong made big strides and he did that. In his one start, in Johannesburg, the 23-year-old not only out-scrummaged the highly rated Tendai Mtawarira, he contributed well around the park, blocking down a kick to set up Jamie Heaslip's try in the second half, which briefly stemmed the Boks' resurgence. By rights Furlong should have started the final Test but for the fact that Schmidt feels Ross offers significantly less value off the bench than as a starter – a little unfair to Furlong, but them's the breaks. Besides, he should get plenty of opportunity in coming seasons.

The other big winner was Paddy Jackson, who proved that he has the temperament as well as the talent to succeed Sexton as Ireland's first-choice playmaker. There were wobbles along the way – a restart that went out on the full in Cape Town, an intercept pass in the same game, a poor option at a critical moment in Port Elizabeth. But each time, Jackson's next contribution was positive – a key indicator of mental strength. He also place-kicked beautifully, passed sharply and defended like a demon.

Speaking of defence, another major plus from the tour was the influence of the newly arrived Andy Farrell, so evident especially in the first Test, when Ireland's line speed was noticeably more aggressive than it had been in the Six Nations and when they gang-tackled with a determination which rattled the Boks in midfield especially. Farrell brought a new energy and a new voice and already he has put himself at the head of the queue to succeed Schmidt.

Other positives? We saw the re-emergence of Luke Marshall, who blew a try-scoring chance in Port Elizabeth but was otherwise excellent. Stuart Olding justified the coach's faith in him and is now a viable option at 12. This made it easier for Henshaw to move one slot wider to outside centre, where he looks so much more dangerous, which in turn allowed Payne to play two Tests at full back, where he can have greatest influence.

The absence of Payne and Henshaw for the final Test heaped even more pressure on a tiring squad and yet they would have won but for a couple of botched opportunities, the dominance of the Boks' scrum and some heroic Bok defence, especially by their diminutive scrum half, Faf de Klerk. Schmidt might have complained about the match officials' decision to show Willie le Roux a yellow card for his challenge on O'Halloran, when many observers believed it had been more reckless than Stander's in Cape Town. The Kiwi was more disappointed about missed opportunities in attack – but still managed to be philosophical about what had been achieved on tour.

'If you'd said to me before we came here: "Look, there'll be three six-point results and you'll get one of them" I would have grabbed it. I'm not sure the players would have, because they are so committed to trying to justify the support they get. But I thought they did a super job, and I think they'll learn from it. But you can't spend too much time learning. You've got to get to the level of mastering very, very quickly in this environment because you don't get too many windows to play Test rugby in a season and you've got to optimise every window you get.'

Schmidt made sure to pay tribute to Eoin Reddan, who departed professional rugby after a glittering career which earned him 71 Test caps and several medals for Leinster and Wasps. Typically, Reddan was at the heart of Ireland's late assault in Port Elizabeth, scurrying from ruck to ruck as the tourists went in search of the score that might have nicked the result. It wasn't to be, but Ireland will be stronger – and wiser – for the experience.

HOME FRONT

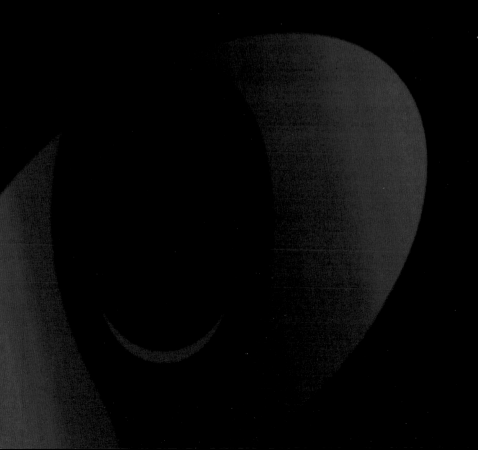

Quietly Does It
Mark McCall and Sarries' Success Story
by CHRIS JONES

'Venter laid the foundations for the Sarries success – their first Aviva Premiership title came in 2011 – but it has been McCall who has overseen a remarkably consistent run of titles'

Five years ago Brendan Venter told Mark McCall that he would be quitting Saracens and heading back to his GP practice outside Cape Town. While the former Springbok World Cup winner would continue to be a technical director, the Saracens ship was now under McCall's command.

It was assumed the club would need time to adjust to the quietly spoken McCall after the headline-grabbing antics of Venter, who enjoyed tweaking the noses of those in power. Little did we realise that not only would the transfer of the director of rugby role be seamless, it was also going to take the North London club to the very summit of European rugby.

Venter laid the foundations for the Sarries success – their first Aviva Premiership title came in 2011 – but it has been McCall who has overseen a remarkably consistent run of titles that has elevated the club to a European Champions Cup and Premiership double in 2016. Sarries reinforced the view that they are the team to beat by retaining their Premiership title having finished in the top four of the English league for a seventh successive season. They also won the LV= Cup last year with a team captained by a young man called Maro Itoje!

However, McCall and his players had to suffer considerable pain before the elation of double triumph, having learned from the dark days of 2014 when they lost to Toulon in the European Cup final and then endured an extra-time loss in the Premiership final to Northampton. McCall said: 'We all remember what it felt like two years ago when we lost two finals in a row, the second of them in the last second of extra time. It was painful and as hard as it gets.

'You can only play 33 games in a season and we lost four last season. That's not a bad record and it indicates that we don't pick and choose our games, but front up all the time. If we keep that up I don't see why we won't be back in these sorts of games. The age profile of the squad is good, is really good.

'Everybody is signed up for the next two to three seasons. The spine of the team is there, but the Premiership is always getting better. We've got to stay hungry and motivated and no doubt we will.'

Those young players included Itoje, Owen Farrell, George Kruis, plus Mako and Billy Vunipola, all of whom enjoyed remarkable seasons at club and international level. They helped the club dominate Europe, powered England to Grand Slam glory and then to an historic first Test series win in Australia. The Sarries effect has been all-consuming.

Allied to those players were the talents of Alex Goode, the Premiership Player of the Season, the incredibly consistent form of wing Chris Wyles, the USA captain, combined with the try-scoring maverick play of Chris Ashton on the other flank. Scotland centre Duncan Taylor had a storming season alongside Brad Barritt – the rock of the team – while the retiring Charlie Hodgson and scrum halves Richard Wigglesworth and Neil de Kock put into play the tactical plan that McCall is so good at formulating with his fellow coaches. One week McCall was overseeing the defeat of eventual French champions Racing 92 in the European final and the next he was helping the players with tactics to overcome Exeter in the Premiership final at Twickenham.

ABOVE Mark McCall (right) watches Saracens win the 2011 Aviva Premiership final against Leicester at Twickenham, alongside then technical director Brendan Venter.

FACING PAGE McCall (left) and long-time backer and chairman Nigel Wray celebrate Sarries' 2016 European Champions Cup final win in Lyon.

Venter is not surprised by McCall's success and has always believed he made the right choice as the club's next director of rugby, a position that had been filled by many others – including Eddie Jones – before the South African arrived to provide stability in 2009. Venter said: 'This is not the culmination of seven years' work – it is the beginning of something awesome if you look at the players at the club.

'I often joked with Mark about the different styles of leadership at Sarries. Myself and Andy Farrell were the extrovert leaders, jumping up and down shouting while he was quiet. Being an introvert leader is sometimes better because you hear other people's opinions. The dominant leader doesn't always hear other views.

'The future is amazing because the guys could be together for another six to eight years and players like Maro Itoje, Jamie George, George Kruis and Owen Farrell could finish their careers having been in one place for ten years. It is achievable.'

Venter played alongside McCall at London Irish in 1998 in a back line that would produce four Premiership directors of rugby. Besides the two Sarries men, Conor O'Shea was full back and has just ended six years in charge of Harlequins to coach Italy while the outside half was David Humphreys, the current Gloucester DOR.

McCall's success will see his name mentioned when Joe Schmidt decides to end his time as Ireland coach, but Venter is confident his friend will want to take Sarries to the next level. 'It was remarkable to have four directors of rugby in the same back division and I really enjoyed playing alongside Mark,' added Venter. 'Mark loves coaching and it has taken him a long time to build what has been achieved at Sarries and why would he leave something so exciting? It is not how Mark functions.'

Leicester won four Premiership titles from 1999 to 2002 and three more between 2007 and 2010, while Wasps won three consecutive English titles 2003-2005. Sarries' next target will be to retain their domestic and European crowns next season, something Leicester did in 2002.

McCall believes the coaching stability since 2009 has been vital to the club's success and has no intention of going anywhere. 'If you look at Saracens' history prior to Brendan in ten years' professional rugby to that point they had 12 directors of rugby. The history of our club suggests that continuity is the way forward.'

As he basked in the glory of that win over Racing 92, McCall reflected on just how much sacrifice had been made to achieve a European Cup triumph and he is always quick to deflect attention from himself. It is not in McCall's nature to court the limelight and he is much happier to operate on the edges of rugby celebrity. It is a state of mind he wants others to embrace, as prima donnas are not welcome in the Sarries dressing room.

He explained after the Racing 92 win: 'We have got a tightness and a togetherness in this group. Hopefully if we are humble enough, which I think we are, and hungry enough, which I know we are, then there will be more days like this ahead.

'I am just so chuffed for a lot of people. I am chuffed for the players who have worked so hard – not just this year but in previous years. I am chuffed for the staff and for [Saracens chairman] Nigel Wray who has put his heart and soul in to the club for 20 years, it is wonderful to finally give him the big prize at the end.'

McCall asked Tony McCoy, the brilliant jockey, to address the team as they built towards an amazing end to the season and they also headed to Dubrovnik for one of their famous team bonding trips to prepare for their assault on the double. That's right, he let the players enjoy some down time even though it ate into the week leading up to a massive game.

'This is something this club has really fostered over the time I have been here,' he said. 'I wasn't instrumental in that, other people were. But what I have learnt over these last seven seasons with the club is that rugby is not like cycling, for example, where the margins are so fine.

'I understand now that the intangibles are as important as some of the stuff you do in the gym and on the pitch and that togetherness and the relationships you can forge on those trips are as important. The thing about this group is that we trust each other. I trust the players 100 per cent.'

And the Sarries players implicitly trust their quietly spoken director of rugby who deserves all the plaudits – even if he is uncomfortable receiving them!

For business.
For family.
For life.

Wealth is made of much more than money – it is realising hopes and dreams, passions and partnerships. At Arbuthnot Latham we strive to see beyond the obvious to help you achieve what really matters.

t: 020 7012 2500   arbuthnotlatham.co.uk

A Tale of Tenacity
Bristol Return to the Premiership

by NEALE HARVEY

'Undaunted, Bristol went again last season, topping the table in style before finally reaching their Holy Grail after despatching battling Doncaster over two legs'

In October 2010, Bristol Rugby was staring into the abyss. A run-down team was playing second-rate rugby in front of dwindling crowds at a dilapidated Memorial Stadium; finances had collapsed to the point where players were forced to accept 50 per cent pay cuts; and, having failed to win promotion back to the Premiership the previous May, hard-pressed chairman Chris Booy predicted a lengthy spell in the Championship unless new investment was found.

In an interview with the *Rugby Times* that month, Booy declared: 'We have to be honest with our supporters and people must understand the position we are in. We're paying for the legacy of trying to be a Premiership club and for now we have to try to balance the books as best we can.

ABOVE David Lemi lifts the Greene King IPA Championship trophy at Ashton Gate after Bristol had seen off Doncaster Knights to return to the Premiership at last.

'That's a difficult task so we're going to be in the Championship for certainly a couple of years, possibly longer, until such a time as either somebody wants to invest more to give us another shot or that we emerge from our difficult position, get out of the recession and then have a go under our own steam. We continue to look for those new backers and we've spoken to some very wealthy people, but we haven't found the right person yet.'

Booy added: 'In my view, you've got to have come from the area and have passion for it, but we haven't met anybody who's ticked those boxes. This person probably doesn't live in Bristol anymore because we'd have already found him, so by definition we have to widen our search. But we do need to find him quickly because otherwise the future is grim.'

They proved prophetic words, for later that season it emerged that once-proud Bristol were facing extinction. Efforts to find a benefactor had proved fruitless and administration loomed – a mystifying state of affairs for one of English rugby's most famous old clubs, situated in the country's sixth-largest city with a population catchment area in excess of one million.

At the eleventh hour came salvation, however, in the shape of Steve Lansdown, the billionaire owner of Bristol City Football Club who arrived on his white charger with the vision of creating Bristol Sport, an umbrella organisation encompassing football, rugby, basketball, badminton and motor sport that would harness the untapped potential of a city that had massively underachieved on a sporting level. But it came with a proviso: Bristol Rugby had to move to Ashton Gate.

Leaving the Memorial Stadium, Bristol's home since 1921, was anathema to some dyed-in-the-wool fans for whom the thought of crossing south of the River Avon to watch their team was as appealing as lying on a bed of nails. But money talked and common sense prevailed as it became obvious that without Lansdown's cash injection, Bristol Rugby had no top-flight future.

Bristol failed to clinch promotion in 2012, 2013 and 2014. However, backed by Lansdown's millions and with former England head coach Andy Robinson now at the helm, the move to Ashton Gate proceeded in season 2014-15 and supporters responded to the new sense of purpose by turning out in far greater numbers than they had at the Memorial Stadium. Average crowds of 8000, nearly double those at their spiritual home, saw Bristol top the Championship table after 22 rounds, only to be denied in the controversial play-offs by Worcester after two titanic matches – the fourth time in six seasons Bristol had failed in this way.

Undaunted, Bristol went again last season, topping the table in style before finally reaching their Holy Grail after despatching battling Doncaster over two legs to ensure a return to the Premiership after seven long years outside English rugby's elite. The second match at Ashton Gate attracted a full-house 16,000 and with capacity at the impressively refurbished stadium set to reach 27,000 this season, Bristol Rugby can legitimately anticipate matching the Premiership's big-hitters in terms of crowds and trophy-winning potential.

Bullish Booy, who is targeting average attendances of 15,000, said: 'We now have the best club rugby stadium in the country and we're about to embark on creating a new state-of-the-art training centre, so we have ambitions to be competing at the top end of the Premiership and Europe.

'Clearly it will take time, but we have the resources and supporter base to do that and "boom and bust" is over financially. Steve Lansdown's committed to this project long-term and we know that because of what he's done at Bristol City over a number of years. He's not a quitter, he's determined to see this project through.

'It'll be tough next season. Every year the Premiership gets better and we're coming late to the party, but we'll work hard to improve our squad. Our expectation this season is not to get relegated and we'll have a strategy around that while we recruit what we need in parallel to move on. With

ABOVE After so many disappointments, director of rugby Andy Robinson savours Bristol's moment of promotion glory after the play-off final.

FACING PAGE Ashton Gate, home of Bristol City FC, ready for Bristol Rugby to entertain Moseley in the GKIPA Championship in February 2015, the season the rugby club moved into the ground.

ABOVE Bristol full back Luke Arscott crosses for a disallowed try during the 2010 Championship play-off final first leg against Exeter Chiefs. Arscott is now back at Bristol after stints at Exeter and Bath.

FACNG PAGE Samoa international Tusi Pisi, who joined Bristol in 2016-17, takes on the Southern Kings on behalf of the Sunwolves in 2016 Super Rugby.

the constraint of being in the Championship gone, we can compete for the best players.'

For his part, Lansdown is delighted to be helping Bristol Rugby become great again. A local businessman who made his fortune in financial services, he has lofty ambitions of creating a sporting Mecca to match those of London, Liverpool and Manchester.

Lansdown explained: 'My main sporting passion is football and I've been involved with Bristol City now for over 20 years, so yes that's first and foremost. But the idea of bringing a number of sports together under one banner in Bristol Sport was formulated from that and is gradually being developed.

'Bristol's been a sporting backwater for many years and one thing that always grated with me was the fact that people always took the mickey out of it. Certain comments grate and in my own way I wanted to try to prove them wrong. There's passion for sport here – let's bring it to the forefront, shout about it and make it even more successful.'

Lansdown added: 'Bristol Rugby financially had significant debts and basically it was minutes from going out of business really. We didn't make a lot of fuss about it at the time, but we had all the papers in place for administration.

'But Bristol is a rugby hotbed and if you saw the crowd for our last game against Doncaster, it proved what potential there is. If you look down the road at Exeter and what they've achieved, that's what we're aiming to do now.'

With Lansdown's huge backing and all that potential, how can Bristol possibly fail? Well, for starters the Premiership is a much tougher, physical and mentally more gruelling league than the one Bristol left behind in 2009 and Robinson, a hard-nosed former Bath back-rower who has also coached the British & Irish Lions and Scotland, knows the challenge ahead.

He said: 'The hard work starts – we want to perform well in the Premiership and there are a lot of improvements we've got to make. The players and management put in an incredible effort to make sure that we got promoted and now we have to stay there.

'We'll bring a lot to the Premiership this year and the rest of the Premiership will enjoy coming to Ashton Gate. We look forward to Bath coming this season, Gloucester, Exeter too, and we believe we can sell out at 27,000, which will be great for the league.'

Changes to the coaching team have seen assistant coach Sean Holley depart, while former Wales scrum half Dwayne Peel has been added to the back-room staff as attack coach along with another ex-Wales star Jonathan Thomas (defence) and Mark Bakewell (forwards).

Recruitment remains ongoing, but Samoan fly half Tusi Pisi has arrived from Super Rugby along with experienced former England No. 8 Jordan Crane from Leicester. Ex-Scarlets pair Jordan and Rhodri Williams are on board, as is Nick Fenton-Wells, the former Saracens back-rower who spent last season at Championship rivals Bedford, while full back Luke Arscott has signed from Bath and back-rower Jon Fisher from Northampton.

Said Robinson: 'We've got work to do, but we believe we have a Premiership squad and we'll aim to compete hard. The faith Chris Booy, Steve Lansdown and the management team have put in me has been tremendous; they've done a fantastic job over the last ten years and the backing we've received from our supporters has been equally incredible. With that backing we believe we can be successful and that's what I'll be aiming for.'

From being a financial basket case five years ago, Bristol now have the capability to realise the potential of a city that has been crying out to make an impact in top-level professional sport. Could this be their time? If they can get through their first season back in the top flight without being relegated, they appear to have every chance.

'This is just the start,' insists Booy. 'Bristol Rugby has the ambition to win trophies at the highest level of the game and we won't rest until we achieve that.'

Booy can put his old begging bowl away. Bristol are back!

Montpellier Hold Firm
the European Challenge Cup

by HUGH GODWIN

'Quins introduced Kyle Sinckler, Dave Ward and Jack Clifford from the bench, but another penalty conceded in the scrum emphasised the edge Montpellier were enjoying'

The Anglo-French takeover of the European Champions Cup in 2015-16 was echoed in the competition's junior partner, as Harlequins met Montpellier to contest the final of the Challenge Cup in Lyon.

It represented a rapid reunion of the two clubs after they had scored a home win each in two meetings during the pool stage. In round one in November, Harlequins won 41-18 at the Stoop, accumulating six tries against a Montpellier team whose head coach Jake White had recruited a hefty battalion of seven South African compatriots – including three of the Springboks he coached to win the 2007 World Cup – to bolster an already cosmopolitan squad. For the round-six rematch in January, White picked a stronger starting line-up and Montpellier won 42-9 with five tries in the south of France, but the Quins from southwest London could argue justifiably they were short of motivation as they had secured qualification for the quarter-finals beforehand, with five bonus-point victories including wins home and away against Cardiff Blues and the Italians of Calvisano.

In the knockout rounds, Harlequins came through two home matches fairly comfortably, with wins over London Irish (38-30) and Grenoble (30-6) respectively. Montpellier, more eye-catchingly, won 25-19 away to Sale in the quarter-finals, thereby inflicting a first defeat on the Sharks at the AJ Bell Stadium since Harlequins won there in April 2015. In their semi-final, Montpellier built a 22-point lead at home to Newport Gwent Dragons, and eventually prevailed 22-12 over the Welsh team who had knocked out the cup holders Gloucester in the previous round.

All of which added up to a form guide pointing marginally towards Montpellier as the finalists and their supporters converged on Lyon in mid-May. Following the pattern set by the tournament organisers in Cardiff in 2011, the final of the Challenge Cup on the Friday night would be followed by the corresponding showdown for the Champions Cup in the same city the next day. For the first time, though, one stadium would stage both matches – in this case, the brand-new, 60,000-capacity Grand Stade on the eastern outskirts of France's capital of gastronomy.

Harlequins travelled in a subdued mood after receiving the awful news a few days beforehand that Seb Adeniran-Olule, a highly promising 20-year-old prop who had made three appearances in the first team, had died in a car crash. The club had also recently confirmed the long-rumoured departure of director of rugby Conor O'Shea to take charge of Italy. This would be the voluble Irishman's final match after six years at the Stoop, which included a Premiership title in 2012. Among the Quins replacements, the New Zealander fly

FACING PAGE Akapusi Qera, Montpellier's Fiji back-row, feels the full force of Harlequins' Joe Marler during the European Challenge Cup final in Lyon.

BELOW Jack Clifford, recently capped by England in the 2016 Six Nations, offloads against London Irish in the Challenge Cup quarter-final at the Stoop, which Quins won 38-30.

half Ben Botica was in the odd position of preparing to face the club he had just agreed to join for the subsequent season.

There was little mystery about the Harlequins team – Mike Brown, George Lowe, Nick Evans, Danny Care, Joe Marler, Chris Robshaw, Luke Wallace and Nick Easter formed a long-serving core, while the comparative newcomers Jamie Roberts, Tim Visser, Adam Jones and James Horwill were all hardened veterans of the international game. Quins knew the specific task at hand well, too, having won the Challenge Cup in 2001, 2004 and 2011, on each occasion against French opposition.

By contrast Montpellier's only previous European final was a win in the now defunct, third-tier Shield competition in 2004. But they were heading for an impressive third-place finish in the Top 14, and despite their France fly half François Trinh-Duc being absent injured, the presence of Springboks of the calibre of Frans Steyn, Pierre Spies and the front-row du Plessis brothers, plus the Fiji flanker Akapusi Qera and Australia scrum half Nic White, negated any notion that a team containing only three French-qualified players might be overawed.

Evans nudged Harlequins ahead with a penalty, before his fly-half counterpart Demetri Catrakilis (one of the South African septet) replied in kind. Evans hit a post with a penalty from medium range in the 12th minute, then Montpellier lost their full back Benjamin Fall to a hamstring injury as he chased back in defence. This proved to be a blessing in disguise, as Montpellier built on a bullocking break by the big lock Paul Willemse to fashion a sweeping try finished in the left corner by Fall's Australian replacement, Jesse Mogg, after Quins' England wing Marland Yarde was discombobulated by the footwork and interplay of Marvin O'Connor and the 34-year-old former All Black centre, Anthony Tuitavake. The conversion by Catrakilis was followed by a penalty goal from the same player for a lead of 13-3 with 28 minutes gone as Harlequins tried illegally to halt a driving maul. The Montpellier pack had forced the earlier penalty at a scrum, and this hard-eyed bunch were living up to a formidable reputation.

The gap was reduced to a more manageable four points before half-time, as Evans kicked two penalties for Harlequins. There was also a questionable dive into a ruck by Marler, the England prop who was making his return from suspension after kicking a Grenoble opponent in the semi-final, but the referee Johnny Lacey took no action. At this stage Quins were ahead in terms of territory and possession, but a golden chance to increase the pressure was lost three minutes into the second half when Evans pushed a 30-metre penalty kick wide of the posts, after a deliberate knock-on.

ABOVE Montpellier's replacement full back Jesse Mogg celebrates outleaping Jamie Roberts to score his second try of the final.

FACING PAGE Bismarck du Plessis dives over for his side's only try as Montpellier record a 22-12 win in their home semi-final against the Dragons.

Emboldened by that let-off, Montpellier kicked a penalty for a line out on the Quins 22-metre line, and mauled their way into the midfield. A few phases later Qera was tackled near the goal line, and with a penalty advantage to fall back on, the substitute scrum half Benoît Paillaugue cross-kicked to Mogg who outjumped Jamie Roberts at the right-hand corner and maintained control adroitly to ground the ball for a try as he landed. The ineffectual leap by Roberts was not a moment for the experienced Welshman to remember fondly.

Catrakilis added a tricky conversion and the 26-year-old from Johannesburg with Greek-Cypriot roots kept punishing Quins with penalties in the 56th and 68th minutes to put Montpellier 26-9 up, as rain began to teem down. The run of play was by no means one-sided, but a fumble by Sam Twomey at an attacking line out in the Montpellier 22, and a kick-pass from Brown that was dropped by Visser with a try looming, were further blows to Harlequins' morale. They introduced Kyle Sinckler, Dave Ward and Jack Clifford from the bench to revitalise the pack, but another penalty conceded in the scrum emphasised the edge Montpellier were enjoying, and Quins were rarely able to mount their familiar offloading movements in the face of a well-drilled defence who turned every ruck into a titanic physical contest.

The closing stages were a mix of the brilliant and the baffling. Evans was replaced by Botica, one Kiwi for another, and the new man was charged with saving the day against his future team-mates.

Bursts by Robshaw and Lowe stretched the blanket of Montpellier white jerseys to breaking point, and Brown's dainty grubber with the outside of the boot bounced nicely for Yarde, who kept his wits amid a double tackle to score on the left wing. Botica converted and his subsequent penalty in front of the posts left Quins with just over two minutes to find the converted try they needed to tie the scores.

Given Quins' history in Europe of playing hard to the final whistle, their obduracy as they chased an unlikely comeback was no surprise, and a tremendous tackle by Marler on Qera helped turn possession over in the Montpellier half. But it was not maintained as Sinckler was penalised for holding on after a tackle, with O'Connor jackalling for the ball over the tight-head prop. And that was followed by the final indignity – a horrendous misjudgment by Botica as he kicked the ball downfield and into Montpellier's grateful hands with the clock having ticked beyond the regulation 80 minutes. The ball was duly booted into touch for the end of the match, a distraught Botica berated himself, beating the turf in frustration; and the winning captain, the France flanker Fulgence Ouedraogo, made ready to collect the trophy.

'We're tremendously disappointed but we must give credit to Montpellier, they put us under pressure and squeezed us early on,' said Robshaw, while O'Shea was understandably reflective, as his team's run of six winning finals in all competitions came to an end and they missed out on qualification for next season's Champions Cup. 'We fought to the bitter end, and for that I am proud,' O'Shea said. 'The team should be hugely proud of what they achieved in the six years I have been with them. It is a very special group of people, and I have been lucky to have the opportunity.'

For his part, Jake White took Montpellier's win as a sign of greater things to come. 'I am really happy, because this group of players now understands just how tough it is to win something. Maybe it's not the Champions Cup, but next year we will be playing in the Champions Cup, and that will be a great measurement, playing the likes of Saracens, Leinster and Munster.'

RIGHT Montpellier, European Challenge Cup winners 2016, celebrate at the Grand Stade de Lyon.

Your *nest egg* could become a valuable source of income PROFITS.

Fig. 1:
An ordinary nest egg

Fig. 2:
A more valuable nest egg

FOR YEARS, cracking open your retirement nest egg and converting it into an annuity was your only option. But following the changes in the law last year, you can now fashion your nest egg into a valuable source of income Profits. Of course few know more about these gems than the Artemis hunters. We have expertise in income both at home and abroad. From both bonds and equities. And in each case, our hunters have a glittering reputation. The decision to access your pension savings is an extremely important one. Before you do so, Artemis strongly advises you to seek advice from a financial adviser to help you to understand your options. Please remember that past performance should not be seen as a guide to future performance. The value of an investment and any income from it can fall as well as rise as a result of market and currency fluctuations and you may not get back the amount originally invested.

ARTEMIS
The PROFIT Hunter

0800 092 2051   investorsupport@artemisfunds.com   artemis.co.uk

Unbeatable Saracens
the European Champions Cup

by DAVID HANDS

'It has taken the best part of 20 years for the sustained belief and investment of their chairman, Nigel Wray, to bring Saracens to the grandest club stage of all'

T his was a season of European rugby like no other. Both European cup campaigns were compressed by the staging of the eighth World Cup in England, but the opening weekend of competition was marred by terrorist atrocities in Paris. Then, when the European Rugby Champions Cup concluded with an English win on French soil, it rounded off something of a renaissance for the game in England.

Few seriously expected, after watching the national side limp out of their home World Cup during the pool stage, that three English clubs would reach the semi-finals of the Champions Cup. Yet there were Saracens, Leicester and Wasps contending with Racing 92 for a place in the final at Lyon, and how well deserved was the 21-9 win

ABOVE Racing 92's Alexandre Dumoulin is brought crashing to earth in the driving rain by Duncan Taylor as Saracens set about claiming their first European title in Lyon.

achieved by Saracens over Racing at the Grand Stade de Lyon. Disregard the critics who sought to underline the limitations of the Saracens game: this is a team for all seasons who should continue to be a dominant force in Europe.

It is, though, pertinent to wonder to what degree French involvement was knocked sideways by terrorist attacks outside the Stade de France and at a rock concert in the Bataclan theatre which left 130 dead and more than 350 injured. While the Champions Cup was kicking off on 13 November at Welford Road between Leicester and Stade Français, events unfolding in Paris left sport way down the list of anyone's priorities; the French government called off sporting fixtures in the wake of the attacks, which left five matches to be rearranged. French teams playing abroad, which included Toulouse at Saracens, were given the option of postponement, and though Toulouse decided to honour the fixture, their thoughts may well have been elsewhere.

Though sport can surely help revival of national spirit, it was no surprise to find French clubs struggling for consistency as the Champions Cup progressed. For three years, Toulon had been supreme in Europe in an unprecedented run of success. Now their first match in defence of the title, a week after the terrorist attacks, came against Wasps in Coventry where their luminaries revealed unexpected feet of clay in the 32-6 defeat which suggested the glory days of a decade earlier could be on the way back for Wasps.

But, in a campaign which brought them a cherished double of domestic and European titles, this season belonged to Saracens. It has taken the best part of 20 years, from the dawn of professional rugby, for the sustained belief and investment of their chairman, Nigel Wray, to bring them to the grandest club stage of all; but now they are there, all the signs suggest they will be hard to dislodge. En route they have played pragmatic rugby, as they did in heavy rain in the final against

ABOVE Argentine flyer Juan Imhoff, a member of Racing 92's star-studded back division, gives the Leicester defence the slip in the semi-final at Nottingham. All Black maestro Dan Carter, who kicked 11 points in Racing's victory, gives support.

LEFT Charles Piutau crosses in the 79th minute against the Chiefs. Jimmy Gopperth duly converted to launch Wasps into the semi-finals.

Racing, but year on year they have added layers to their game.

Along the way they helped provide the backbone of the England side that, in 2016, recovered from the depths of World Cup despair to win the Six Nations Grand Slam. Maro Itoje, their young back-five forward, became European Player of the Year, their defence coach (Paul Gustard) and former captain (Steve Borthwick) joined the England staff, but they handled their resources splendidly; after the disappointment of losing the 2014 European final, they went through the 2015-16 Champions Cup calendar unbeaten, the first club ever to do so.

Moreover, given their well-established connections with South Africa, Saracens will be intrigued that European Professional Club Rugby, the governing body for the Champions Cup, confirmed in March negotiations with their southern-hemisphere counterparts, SANZAR, for a meeting of the champions of each hemisphere. There have been efforts before to bring together the

Super Rugby champions and the Heineken Cup holders, which have come to nothing, but any sensible discussion around a global season for the game would include such a clash.

That is for the future. The pacemakers in 2015-16 were undoubtedly Wasps, for whom Charles Piutau, their New Zealand wing, ended the tournament having made more clean breaks, and more ground, than anyone else. He was a try scorer in the 33-6 demolition in Dublin of Leinster, three times champions between 2009 and 2012, at the beginning of a depressing year for the Irish provinces in the Champions Cup. When Wasps followed that up with that cracking win over Toulon, which included two tries from Nathan Hughes, their No. 8, everyone took notice.

Meanwhile, Racing, who had signed Dan Carter, New Zealand's World Cup-winning fly half, started with a bonus-point win over the Scarlets in Llanelli before ceding the stage, in the third round, to Exeter Chiefs. The West Country club, having only reached England's elite in 2010, had no European hinterland of which to speak and few would have placed much money on them beating the giants of Clermont Auvergne, even at Sandy Park. But beat them they did, recovering from an early 11-point deficit to score four tries through their forwards and come away with a 31-14 success. Given the absence through injury of four key players, it was an epic display.

Glasgow, too, offered an emphatic performance in beating Scarlets 43-6, helped by three tries from the Fijian-born wing Taqele Naiyaravoro. In the same pool, Carter made his much-anticipated debut at the Stade Yves-du-Manoir as Racing dismissed Northampton 33-3, though it was a game noticeable for the contribution from the Saints back row of Teimana Harrison, capped by England at the season's end.

There was, though, a road bump for Wasps when they lost at home to Bath. Three different kickers registered six penalty goals to edge Wasps' noses in front but, in time added on, they were reduced by yellow cards to 14 then 13 men, and Anthony Watson scored a try in the corner which, with George Ford's conversion, gave Bath their 25-23 win. But in an unmemorable season for Bath, it did not last and a week later they lost 36-10 to Wasps, for whom Elliot Daly, the centre, was inspirational.

If Wasps were doing well, so were Leicester. Even when Munster are out of sorts, an away win at Thomond Park remains worthy of celebration, and the Tigers became the first visitors to win two European ties there with a 31-19 triumph. They backed that up by beating the Irish province 17-6 at Welford Road, which virtually ensured a quarter-final place with two rounds to go.

The final two rounds of pool play, though, brought both glory and controversy. The glory belonged to Exeter, who to reach the last eight for the first time needed to beat the Ospreys, leaders of Pool Two, by at least 13 points and then hope that Bordeaux-Bègles won at Clermont. The Chiefs did their part, winning 33-17, then heard that Bordeaux had won 37-28 and that Morgan Parra, the Clermont scrum half, had turned down an easy penalty which would have earned a losing bonus point and cost Exeter qualification.

The controversy attended Saracens. They beat Ulster 33-17 at Allianz Park, but then discovered that Chris Ashton, the wing recalled to England's training squad, would be cited for making contact with the eye area of Luke Marshall, the Ulster centre. Ashton declared his innocence, but the subsequent investigation imposed a ten-week suspension, leaving him unavailable to England throughout the Six Nations.

LEFT A delighted Mako Vunipola as Saracens are awarded a 72nd-minute penalty try against Wasps in the semi-final at Reading's Madejski Stadium. The score, converted by Owen Farrell, gave Sarries a big enough cushion to see off Wasps' late surge.

ABOVE Owen Farrell lines up a kick against Racing 92 in the final. The fly half kicked seven penalties to Johan Goosen's three to bring Sarries a 21-9 victory – and the cup.

That left two all-England quarter-finals, one Anglo-French encounter, and the meeting in Paris of Racing and Toulon. The goal-kicking of Maxime Machenaud, the scrum half, saw Racing home 19-16, while Leicester offered probably the definitive performance of their season with a 41-13 win over Stade Français, reaching the last four for the first time in seven years. Saracens, more lethargic than they would have wished, trailed Northampton for much of the game but steadied themselves (helped by a try from Ashton) to win 29-20.

The edge-of-the-seat display was reserved for Coventry's Ricoh Arena where Wasps, thanks to the last kick of the match from Jimmy Gopperth, won 25-24 against Exeter. Gopperth's kicking gave Wasps an early advantage, but two tries by Thomas Waldrom pushed Exeter ahead, and going into the final quarter the Chiefs led 24-11. But Wasps held their nerve; players such as Ashley Johnson and Thomas Young came off the bench to add momentum, and tries by Frank Halai and, at the death, Piutau set the scene for Gopperth's clincher.

The reward for Wasps was a semi-final against Saracens at Reading's Madejski Stadium and an opening try by Dan Robson, their scrum half who enjoyed such a good season. But Saracens have become used to riding out storms. Owen Farrell's kicking gave them a cushion and a driving maul from a line out earned them the penalty try which ensured a 24-17 win and their second appearance in a European final.

Leicester could not make it an all-English final. Playing at the City Ground in Nottingham where they beat Llanelli in the 2002 semi-final, the Tigers were nervy and error-strewn as they went down 19-16 to Racing. Machenaud hurt them with an early try, Carter kicked 11 points, and a long-range effort from Johan Goosen proved the difference after a late try by Telusa Veainu gave a glimmer of hope to Leicester supporters.

It was a first European final for Racing and brought more than 58,000 to Lyon, a ground record. But the wet conditions determined the tactics, and Farrell, in so rich a vein of form, kicked seven penalties to bring the trophy back to England. Many had envisaged the match as a clash of fly halves, Farrell against Carter, but the New Zealander struggled with a calf injury and lasted little more than half the game. In addition, Racing lost Machenaud to a head injury after only 21 minutes, and with him much of their direction.

Goosen kicked two penalties to keep Racing in touch 12-6 at half-time but could only manage a third as Farrell kept punishing the French club's offences, taking his tally for the competition to 127 points, more than any other individual. As much to the point was the game management by Farrell and his half-back partner, Richard Wigglesworth; the threat posed by Chris Masoe and his big pack was neutralised, and though Racing roused themselves in the final quarter in an attempt to retrieve a six-point deficit, their own inaccuracy and an obdurate defence saw Saracens home.

'Two years ago we weren't good enough against Toulon,' Mark McCall, the Saracens director of rugby, said. 'Today was evidence of how we have grown. What we said in the week was that if we stay humble, which we will, and stay hungry, which I know we will, we truly believe there will be more days like this ahead of us.'

Sensational Saracens
the Aviva Premiership

by CHRIS HEWETT

'Delayed by the unfolding of the World Cup pool stage, the Aviva Premiership did not see a pass thrown, a ball kicked or a ribcage rearranged until mid-October'

The English autumn was half over before domestic rugby's rank and file – the folk who buy the season tickets, pay their money at the turnstiles, congregate in the bars and generally give professional union a reason to exist – reached the unavoidable conclusion that Saracens, the reigning champions, would spend the next few months doubling up as repeat champions in waiting. Were the masses a little slow in recognising what Basil Fawlty might have called 'the bleedin' obvious'? Quite the opposite. Delayed by the unfolding of the World Cup pool stage, the Aviva Premiership did not see a pass thrown, a ball kicked or a ribcage rearranged until mid-October. Within minutes of the North Londoners opening their account, those blessed with a functioning pair of eyes knew what was what.

There were no Vunipolas in the Sarries starting line-up at Allianz Park that afternoon; there was no Owen Farrell to kick the goals, or George Kruis to run the line out or Richard Wigglesworth to boss the pack and drop clever little box kicks on the decimal equivalent of a sixpence. Yet they still

put five tries and 41 points past a Sale side who, as the campaign unfolded, would make a strong case for themselves as the most improved team in the country. The holders might just have made a clearer statement of intent had they beaten the 'other' All Blacks, but as Daniel Carter and his fellow silver-ferners had other, grander things on their minds, that opportunity was denied them. The only thing left to them was to marmalise the opposition thrown up by the fixture list. Which they did. In style.

One of the try scorers was a South African flanker by the name of Michael Rhodes, who, when he arrived on these shores from the Cape Town-based Stormers, registered 0.5 on the Richter Scale of Rugby Fame. Over the ensuing months, Rhodes whipped up a storm of serious proportions in the Saracens back row, covering the cracks opened up by Jacques Burger's impending retirement and the quiet but seemingly inexorable demise of a loose forward as capable as Kelly Brown. Not for the first time, or even the twenty-first, the champions had invested in the overseas market and made themselves a packet.

There was a moral underpinning the story and it went something like this: if you're going to spend money, buy something useful with it. While Rhodes was repaying Saracens three times over for the faith they had shown in flying him across the equator, the story at Bath was somewhat different. The West Countrymen,

FACING PAGE For the second time in a fortnight, Brad Barritt lifts a major piece of silverware on behalf of Saracens; this time it is the Aviva Premiership trophy.

ABOVE Sarries back-row Michael Rhodes tackles Lachlan McCaffrey of Leicester Tigers in the semi-final at Allianz Park.

BELOW Exeter Chiefs fly half and ace goal-kicker Gareth Steenson in action during the final at Twickenham.

beaten finalists in 2015 and widely expected to push the Londoners even closer this time around, had splashed bucketloads of hard cash (a cool £500,000 according to many reports) in the direction of the rugby league specialist Sam Burgess, only to see him call time on his new career as a union player the moment England were drummed out of their own World Cup by a lethal combination of Wales, Australia and selectorial cluelessness. It was a numbing experience and it did untold damage down there on the banks of the River Avon, exposing as it did the folly of making a man with zero experience and no obvious position the highest-paid player in the land. As a sporting celebrity, Burgess knocked Rhodes into a cocked hat. As a blind-side flanker, he was not fit to lace the South African's boots. Are we still wondering why Sarries staged a successful defence of their title while their once-closest rivals found themselves slumming it alongside the likes of London Irish, Newcastle and Worcester?

By way of ramming home the point, intelligent things were happening 100 miles southwest of the Georgian city. Exeter, the new best team in the region, headed into the season properly equipped with a recruitment policy fit for purpose, a productive academy system and a squad full to overflowing with players who genuinely wanted to be there. They started with a narrow defeat – at Bath, funnily enough – but it was not long before the likes of Phil Dollman, Ian Whitten, Sam Hill, Will Chudley, Mitch Lees and the outstanding back-rower Don Armand worked up a head of steam. None of these players were particularly well known outside of their own immediate family circles, but they matched the contributions of their higher-profile colleagues – Henry Slade and Luke Cowan-Dickie, Geoff Parling and Dave Ewers and Thomas Waldrom – in delivering results.

And then there was the outside half, goalkicker-in-chief and frequent captain Gareth Steenson, one of the men at the heart of the matter when promotion was achieved in 2010 and still in the thick of it six years on.

LEFT Full back Alex Goode evades the Chiefs defence to touch down in the 75th minute of the final to put Saracens 28-20 ahead. It was the final score of the match.

ABOVE Tommy Taylor – then of Sale, now of Wasps – wrestles with the Leicester defence at Welford Road in a match the Sharks won 10-3.

FACING PAGE London Irish centre Johnny Williams pounces on loose ball to score against Wasps at Twickenham Stadium on double-header day in November 2015.

Across the 24 games from round one to grand final, the Northern Irishman from Dungannon was on the field for all but 14 minutes – not so much a remarkable statistic as a jaw-dropping example of sporting endurance. He was the campaign's top scorer with 258, almost 80 points more than second-placed Jimmy Gopperth of Wasps, and finished just three shy of a century of successful kicks. No one collapsed with shock when the Exeter supporters, who know what they're watching, made him their player of the season.

If the Devonians came up marginally short in the Twickenham decider against opponents far better versed in the ways of the big occasion, they at least spent the second 40 minutes showing the best of themselves to the oval-ball audience. All but paralysed early on – Saracens built a winning lead as a consequence, recording tries by two low-profile but high-value backs in Duncan Taylor and Chris Wyles – the challengers found their way out of a deep freeze of their own construction and ran molten hot for the rest of the encounter, claiming five-pointers of their own through the hooker Jack Yeandle and the hard-working Test wing Jack Nowell before falling to the exquisite sophistication of the England full back Alex Goode at the last knockings.

Saracens' early declaration of superiority and Exeter's impressive speed in establishing themselves as racing certainties for a top-four finish threatened to relieve the league season of much of its tension. Happily, it was not quite a two-horse race: Wasps, proud owners of a licence-to-print-money stadium complex blessed with its own casino and happy to join the Premiership's high-rollers at the big table when it came to recruitment, had secured themselves a sharp attacking edge by signing two New Zealand internationals in Frank Halai and Charles Piutau and availing themselves of a vast reservoir of back-row know-how in the venerable shape of George Smith, the Wallaby flanker of ages past whose performances in the present bordered on the futuristic. Sadly, they flattered to deceive despite these considerable advantages. Any side capable of scoring

64 points at Sarries, as they did in mid-February to the complete astonishment of the world and its wife, were dangerous customers indeed, yet a rough spell of form around Christmas time cost them important points.

Of the also-rans – and we must reluctantly include the once-mighty Leicester among them, despite the significant contributions of the multi-purpose loose forward Lachlan McCaffrey and the electrically charged Tongan wing Telusa Veainu – it was Sale who made the big advance up the mountainside. Danny Cipriani's playmaking skill at outside half was among the chief pleasures of the campaign: but for the horrible ankle injury, suffered in 2008, that cost him the yard of pace that made him such an exhilarating talent, there is no telling what he might have achieved on the international stage. And who is to say that some of the youngsters in the side, from Mike Haley and Sam James among the outside backs to Josh Beaumont and the Wasps-bound Tommy Taylor up front, will not force their way into the Test arena? On the strength of their showing last term, you have to fancy their chances.

Just as it was possible to like the look of the teenaged centre Johnny Williams, despite the poverty of London Irish's relegation-soaked rugby. Williams was nothing short of a rock for the Exiles – a wholly dependable, vibrantly competitive figure who forfeited the chance to play for his country in the Under 20 Six Nations tournament because he understood how much his imperilled club needed him. If he could not quite do enough on his own to maintain the top-flight status of a team playing in the wrong stadium at the wrong point in their development for the wrong reasons, he had no reason to berate himself. Irish could have had a combination of Tim Horan, Ma'a Nonu and Didier Codorniou in the No. 12 shirt and still not stayed up.

Even if the Exiles make an immediate return to the Premiership – no promises, no guarantees – they will be a many a long mile behind the likes of Saracens, Exeter and Wasps: teams who rose above the planning and conditioning disruptions caused by the World Cup and its demands on top talent and found ways of moving forwards at a rate of knots. Not that London Irish are alone in this regard. Some of the biggest, most successful clubs in the country, including some very recent finalists, slipped a long way off the pace last season. Leicester? Northampton? Harlequins? Bath? They have some catching up to do. Lots of it.

next

ARE PROUD TO SUPPORT

THE WOODEN SPOON 2017

REVIEW OF THE
SEASON 2015-16

England Rise Again
the RBS 6 Nations Championship
by CHRIS JONES

'With Jones opting to strip Chris Robshaw of the captaincy and hand it to Hartley – a decision that amazed some – England's new coach quickly set out his stall'

Dylan Hartley was so affected by the concussion he received as England defeated France in their final match in Paris that he probably couldn't work out if he was now captain of the RBS 6 Nations Grand Slam champions or had just won Best of Breed at Crufts!

Hartley did remarkably well to make his way onto the platform and join the rest of the victorious England team in celebrating one of the most significant comebacks in rugby history. The Northampton hooker's rise to national hero mirrored the team's journey from ignominious World Cup failures, who couldn't even get out of their pool despite being tournament hosts, to registering the first England Slam for 13 years.

BELOW Tight-head prop Dan Cole, with former skipper Chris Robshaw in support, goes over for his side's second try in Paris as England overcome France to win a first Six Nations Grand Slam since 2003.

Hartley had not been involved in the cup campaign due to yet another disciplinary problem and by the time the 2015 tournament was over, Stuart Lancaster, the head coach, and his management team were gone. Suddenly, Eddie Jones, an Australian, was the man to impress. With Jones opting to strip Chris Robshaw of the captaincy and hand it to Hartley – a decision that amazed some – England's new coach quickly set out his stall. He would not be constrained by past deeds or reputations and while Robshaw had to deal with no longer being captain, Jones announced the Harlequins forward could become a world-class No. 6, as he was no longer going to be wearing the No. 7 jersey so synonymous with his captaincy under Lancaster.

The changes that Jones instigated included a new coaching team and most importantly a new outlook on the game. Players during the Six Nations talked about the liberating atmosphere Jones engendered, his willingness to let them 'just play', and by opting to pick Bath's George Ford he made it patently clear that while a kicking game would still be a key weapon, the ball needed to be moved through the hands with the No. 10 standing as close to the opposition as possible.

The Jones era started in rather subdued fashion with a hard-fought 15-9 win in Scotland. George Kruis barged over for the first try and then Jack Nowell finished off a great move that featured a behind-the-back pass from Mako Vunipola that highlighted the skills that Jones wanted to utilise throughout the team. Scotland didn't fire and appeared still short of the players to really make an impact, but coach Vern Cotter would find the key to unlocking their potential as the championship unfolded, with full back Stuart Hogg outstanding. France, now under new coach Guy Novès, would be, as usual, unpredictable and they certainly had room for improvement, only scraping past Italy 23-21 in the opening match in Paris, although they did score three tries. It still needed a late penalty from Jules Plisson to clinch victory and he would be one of the players whose inconsistency hurt France in the championship.

Most significantly, Ireland and Wales played out a pulsating 16-16 draw which made for great television but left both coaches, Joe Schmidt and Warren Gatland, to reflect on the fact that neither team could now become Slam champions after just one round of games. Ireland had let a 13-0 lead slip and Rhys Priestland saw his late dropped goal for Wales drift wide.

Ireland looked like they would bounce back with a famous win in Paris, only for Maxime Médard to dart over for the match-winning try late on in the game. Three Sexton penalties gave Ireland a 9-3 lead, but they lost Sean O'Brien, Dave Kearney and Sexton himself to injury in the match, the fly half the victim of an off-the-ball hit by Yoann Maestri.

It was a heartbreaking defeat for the Irish who, as double champions, were just trying to fashion a first win and now saw their hopes of a hat-trick of titles disappear. France won 10-9, with the home fans happy for the victory but still not convinced Novès was improving the performance level. In Rome it was all about how many points England would be scoring once they subdued the Italian team, and it ended 40-9, with Jonathan Joseph grabbing a hat-trick, and Owen Farrell – whose boot would be vital throughout the tournament – racking up 17 points, including a try from a great short pass from Jamie George.

Scotland gave Wales plenty of scares before losing 27-23 in a match that featured one of the great individual tries of recent seasons. George North showed that when he is actually given the ball he remains a force of nature, sidestepping and then sprinting away from the Scottish defence. It was Wales's ninth consecutive win over the Scots, who were proving to be very competitive.

Scotland confirmed this in Rome by defeating Italy 36-20, scoring early and managing to stay ahead of the home side, who were in their final season under Jacques Brunel before Conor O'Shea would take over as head coach for the summer tour of the Americas, having quit Harlequins. If the Scots had lost in Rome it would have been a debilitating tenth Six Nations defeat in a row, and they were relieved to finally taste victory thanks to 21 points from skipper Greig Laidlaw. Italy captain Sergio Parisse was his usual outstanding self, but his side lacked real firepower when it mattered most.

Wales built on their Scotland success by overcoming France 19-10, their fifth successive win over Les Bleus. Dan Biggar scored 14 points for Wales who saw North get another crucial try, while Guilhem Guirado, brilliant throughout the championship, touched down for France. However, the home side had created a vital 13-point lead in the second half and it was enough for the win that set up a title decider with England at Twickenham.

England had also stayed unbeaten by defeating Ireland 21-10 in their first home game under Jones. Conor Murray's try had given the visitors a narrow lead early in the second half before England's territorial domination started to pay off, with tries from Anthony Watson and Mike Brown plus the reliable boot of Farrell doing the trick to the delight of a raucous Twickenham crowd that

had plainly forgotten all about the World Cup losses. England's defence had been excellent and it left the reigning champions winless after three rounds of action. Now it was all about England gaining revenge for that World Cup loss at Twickenham to Wales.

It all started so well for England, with a first-half try from Anthony Watson and three penalties from Owen Farrell putting them 16-0 up at half-time. What could go wrong? The answer was 'a lot' as a charge-down try from Dan Biggar gave Wales hope, followed by two tries in almost as many minutes from North and Taulupe Faletau which left England grimly hanging on to their Slam hopes. North was bundled into touch in the final action of a pulsating game which saw Manu Tuilagi signal his return from long-term injury by helping push the Welsh wing out of play as England won 25-21. They would now head to Paris looking for the Slam to emulate the World Cup-winning team of 2003.

ABOVE The final whistle blows at Murrayfield and Scotland have beaten France 29-18 to the delight of Stuart Hogg (centre), a try scorer in the match.

FACING PAGE Manu Tuilagi saves England's blushes by clattering George North into touch as he threatened to turn a Wales comeback into victory at Twickenham.

They were already installed as Six Nations champions thanks to Scotland's first win over France for ten years as they triumphed 29-18 at Murrayfield with Hogg in stunning form at full back. He made a try for Tim Visser and joined the impressive Duncan Taylor on the try-scoring sheet himself. It was Scotland's biggest win over France for 17 years.

Ireland found their form in an otherwise disappointing campaign with a nine-try 58-15 win over Italy. Andrew Trimble opened the scoring and their pace and precision was just too much for the visitors. It was hardly the kind of performance Italy coach Brunel was hoping for, and his final match would also bring a heavy defeat.

That came against Wales, who took out their frustration on Italy with a thumping 67-14 record-breaking win. Wales secured second place behind England as they scored nine tries on their way to their biggest points total in a championship game in Cardiff. Scrum half Rhys Webb started the rout with the opening try within five minutes, and wing George North scored his fourth try in successive

games. Dan Biggar nipped in for a try in a personal tally of 21 points. There was also a brace for replacement Ross Moriarty. Italy showed some heart in the second half, with scrum half Guglielmo Palazzini and centre Gonzalo Garcia getting tries. Ireland finished the championship in third place courtesy of a four-try-to-three 35-25 victory over Scotland in Dublin. Hogg scored a brilliant solo try for the Scots, but the Irish replied through CJ Stander and Keith Earls. Devin Toner's try with 12 minutes left settled it, but the Scots would not give in and Alex Dunbar got their final try in the 77th minute.

And so attention turned to Paris and one of those late-night kick-offs that ensure a special atmosphere at the Stade de France and endless problems for fans as they try to get the final train/metro back into the city at midnight! There was every reason to hang around celebrating for those England fans in the stadium as a ten-point win allowed Hartley (who was knocked out in the second half making a tackle) to collect the trophy and launch the Jones coaching era with style and substance. However, it wasn't an easy ride for England despite tries from Danny Care and Dan Cole which saw them lead 17-12 at half-time. Maxime Machenaud – who finished with 21 points – kept things tight and despite Watson's third try of the campaign, fingernails were still being bitten by the thousands of English fans in the stadium and millions watching on television. It was entirely appropriate that the European Player of the Year, Maro Itoje, would steal vital French line-out ball late in the game to confirm his emergence as a world-class talent in a team with an average age of just 24.

England and their delirious travelling fans were able to celebrate a 31-21 win and an unbeaten season under Eddie Jones. What a start for the new regime.

The Club Scene
England: Bristol Make the Cut
by NEALE HARVEY

'Having ended the regular season campaign 16 points clear of the field, Andy Robinson's West Country aristocrats were once again made to sweat before they finally crawled over the line'

ABOVE Bristol's Will Cliff scores just before half-time in the second leg of the GKIPA Championship play-off final.

FACING PAGE Action from Richmond v Hartpury College in National One. Hartpury won this encounter 27-21, but Richmond won the return – and promotion.

The Championship play-offs have many critics, amongst them Bristol who consider themselves wholly unfortunate to have been held back by a contrived system that militates against the best side taking its rightful place in the Premiership. As a result, the top flight's hierarchy would be glad to see the back of these end-of-season jousts. But what cannot be argued against is the excitement play-offs create and once again we were treated to some coronary-inducing spectacles.

Having ended the regular season campaign 16 points clear of the field, Andy Robinson's West Country aristocrats were once again made to sweat before – at the fifth time of asking after previously reaching the play-offs in 2010, 2012, 2014 and 2015 – they finally crawled over the line in front of 16,000 tension-ravaged fans at Ashton Gate, defeating Doncaster 60-47 on aggregate to end seven years of hurt and reclaim the place amongst the elite they had forfeited in 2009.

As the Bristol faithful roared their delight at the final whistle, Doncaster's players and management were naturally downcast. They need not have been, however, as South Yorkshire's finest had done themselves proud by reaching that stage just two seasons after returning to the division following a sojourn in National One. Under the wily stewardship of Clive Griffiths, 'Donny' proved they were a match for anyone and they will give relegated London Irish a run this time around. Doncaster put paid to Yorkshire Carnegie's hopes of a return to the Premiership at the semi-final stage, while Bristol accounted for Mike Rayer's Bedford, but the big movers in the Championship last season were Jersey who, under Harvey Biljon's understated stewardship, worked their way into sixth place. Big things are expected of the Channel Islanders this time around, as there will be of London Welsh who demonstrated title-winning form at the end of last season to finish fifth.

At the bottom, the Championship relegation issue turned into a straight shoot-out between Ealing and Moseley, and it was the Midlanders who lost out to end a decade in tier two. Frankly, they were not good enough and the arrival of former Leicester and England lock Louis Deacon as forwards coach in January came too late to reverse the fortunes of Kevin Maggs's underpowered side. Moseley will look to rebuild in National One, while big-spending Ealing can target bigger things.

Bristol's success brought jubilation to the city, and they can now look forward to meeting local rivals Bath, Exeter and Gloucester on equal terms given the huge backing they enjoy from benefactor-in-chief Steve Lansdown. The financial services magnate, who became Bristol's majority shareholder in February 2012, insists there are no limits to what his club can now achieve. Lansdown said: 'We're where we want to be in the Premiership now and that's a huge relief. But we won't rest until we've taken this club to the top end of the league and are competing hard in Europe.'

While Bristol feel they are back where they belong, there was an equally welcome promotion to tier two for Richmond, who have fought their way back up the leagues since being demoted to the bottom rung following the dissolution of the old Premiership side in 1999. Richmond saw off challengers Hartpury College, Blackheath and Ampthill to return to the Championship with a fortnight to spare – the National One title-clinching win at Hartpury leaving head coach Steve Hill in tears.

'I'm just so proud of a very special bunch of guys who have got to the Championship by sheer hard work,' said Hill. 'There are no superstars, no egos, but we showed an awful lot of togetherness this season when things went against us. It's another step and I'm so pleased for our chairman, Peter Moore, who was there when the club needed rescuing 16 years ago. For him to see us going into the Championship must be amazing and we've made lots of people happy.'

However, one thing Richmond will not be doing on their return to the higher echelon is embarking on the kind of wild spending that led to the original club's sad demise.

Hill added: 'We're very clear that we absolutely don't want to do what some clubs do when they get promoted and that is go into the marketplace and recruit a new squad. Yes, there are always, by the nature of things, going to be departures and new arrivals at an "amateur" club and, yes, you look for players who move into the area and might be a good fit.

'But, essentially, we have a good group of players here who have earned this promotion and deserve the opportunity to take on an extremely tough challenge. We will give this our best shot, we will go full bore at it for ten months from when pre-season starts, but nothing will diminish us as a club. We will still have a vibrant, happy club that caters for all standards of rugby from our junior levels right through to the 1st XV.'

Hartpury's achievement in finishing the National One campaign as the twenty-sixth-ranked side in the country cannot be overlooked. A decade ago the college outfit was nowhere to be seen, but their rise has been meteoric and the sheer number of top-class players who have passed through their ranks is unrivalled, with the likes of Jonny May, Ross Moriarty, Tom Savage, Henry Trinder and Alex Cuthbert amongst a host of professionals to have cut their teeth at the club.

The achievement of village side Ampthill in finishing fourth was equally impressive and, under former Wales international Paul Turner, they will again be a threat this season – as will Coventry, who had a poor campaign last time but should prosper under ambitious new head coach Rowland Winter, who joined this summer after steering Cambridge to promotion from level four.

'It's a new challenge and an opportunity to get Coventry, a sleeping giant of National League rugby, to where they want to be,' said Winter. 'Performances haven't been good and the off-pitch support hasn't been good enough either, so there'll be a clear-out. We'll build a new squad and make changes that will enable the club to make the transition towards full-time rugby.'

Meanwhile, new-look Plymouth Albion, under Graham Dawe, performed far better than expected following relegation from the Championship, but were rocked in March when the club went into administration and were deducted 30 points. A second successive relegation was avoided, but the club's new owners dispensed with Dawe's services and former prop Dan Parkes will take the club forward. Albion broke new ground this summer by appointing businesswoman Ali Hannaford as their first female chairman with a remit to transform the club's finances.

Hannaford said: 'We've got a vision of where we want to be, which is in the Premiership, and my focus is on developing income streams to support that. We're looking to build the supporter base and get them behind us, so there'll be some nice surprises for the fans when they return in September. We'll be working hard on sponsorship and running this club as a business, and if the rugby side is successful we'll quickly move ahead with our plans.'

At the foot of National One, Henley and Cinderford found themselves marooned in relegation mire from the outset, and they will be joined in National Two next season by Wharfedale, who succumbed after a 20-year unbroken stay in the third tier of English rugby. They are replaced by Cambridge, who overcame season-long challengers Old Albanians to claim the National Two South title, and Macclesfield, who clinched the Two North title with something to spare.

Old Albanians earned due reward for an excellent points tally by hosting Sedgley Park in the National Two play-off and duly despatched the northerners to reclaim their place in level three. Relegated from National Two North were Sandal, Broadstreet and Huddersfield, while Dorking, Southend and financially stricken and winless Launceston were demoted from Two South. Promoted automatically from National Three were London Irish Wild Geese, Exmouth, Sheffield Tigers and Scunthorpe, while Barnstaple and Hinckley made it up via two thrilling play-offs.

Despite doubts over its future format, the County Championship continues to enthral and Cornwall made it back-to-back wins at Twickenham ahead of England's match against Wales. Around 4000 Cornish fans made the journey, proving passion for the tournament remains fierce, and

ABOVE The RFU Senior Vase final at Twickenham between West Leeds from Yorkshire and Devon club Withycombe, for whom lock forward Dave Sims (far right, in green), formerly of Gloucester, Exeter and England, was appearing in his last match before retiring as a player.

a 35-13 victory over Cheshire sent the hordes back happy across the Tamar to Truro, where the Bill Beaumont Cup was paraded. East Midlands clinched the County Championship Plate, beating Kent 33-27, while Hampshire defeated Staffordshire 33-11 to claim the County Championship Shield.

Lower league cup competitions again proved popular, although this year's finals proved a tad one-sided. Tunbridge Wells defeated St Benedicts 56-14 to lift the RFU Intermediate Cup at Twickenham, while Withycombe succumbed 42-22 at the hands of West Leeds in the Senior Vase and Buxton's long journey from the Peak District ended in a 50-0 Junior Vase final thrashing by Old Cranleighans.

Scotland: RWC, Rain and Residency

by ALAN LORIMER

'A major problem for player development at both Glasgow and Edinburgh is that neither club plays in a reserve league similar to that which shadows the English Premiership'

If expectations of Glasgow Warriors repeating their 2015 Guinness PRO12 success were high, then a quick reassessment was required when Scotland coach Vern Cotter announced his squad for the Rugby World Cup. Warriors supplied more than half of the Scotland World Cup squad, and with insufficient strength in depth to cover the gaps, the Scotstoun club was never able to achieve a level of consistency during and immediately after the period of the global competition. And ultimately that proved significant. To their credit, however, Warriors rallied in the final third of the campaign, winning nine matches in a row to secure a place in the PRO12 play-offs. But against a

strong and inspired Connacht team in the semi-final at Galway, Glasgow could not reproduce their winning form, their hopes of appearing in the PRO12 final at Murrayfield wiped out as the Galway men secured a 16-11 win.

Every cloud, and there are many in Glasgow, has its lining of argentum. Glasgow proved this saying true during the World Cup when, in blooding a number of young players, they discovered exciting new talent. A prime example was their young second-row Scott Cummings, who went on to captain the Scotland Under 20 side. Other uncapped players who featured for Glasgow were centres Sam Johnson and Nick Grigg and the former Newcastle and England Saxons fly half Rory Clegg, signed by Glasgow for the World Cup period and then brought back to Scotstoun on a permanent deal. Opportunities arose too for scrum halves Grayson Hart and Ali Price, both of whom impressed, as well as the young prop D'arcy Rae, who ended the season starting for Glasgow.

If top honours in the Guinness PRO12 evaded Glasgow Warriors, then there was an equal lack of success in the European Rugby Champions Cup. Glasgow's faint chance of qualifying for the knockout stages was blown in the last ten minutes of the return match with Northampton at Franklin's Gardens when their lock Tim Swinson was yellow-carded for foul play, allowing the Saints to overtake Warriors with a late try by their wunderkind Harry Mallinder.

But back to the issue of (or rather, from) clouds. What marred Glasgow's season was, quite simply, rain. Scotstoun flooded badly last season and forced Warriors to migrate to Kilmarnock FC's ground, appropriately called Rugby Park, for several of their fixtures. The plastic surface suited Glasgow's style of play and was perhaps what finally convinced the powers that be within Glasgow City Council that Scotstoun's turf should be replaced by a synthetic pitch, a decision that will allow Warriors to play the expansive running game favoured by their coach, Gregor Townsend.

Despite not achieving the stratospheric heights of their 2014-15 season, Glasgow still outshone their east coast rivals, Edinburgh, who failed to progress in the European Challenge Cup and also finished a lowly ninth in the Guinness PRO12. Edinburgh, however, gained much satisfaction from back-to-back wins over Glasgow during the festive period, but over the season they could not develop a style of exciting rugby that would enthuse their supporters. Even so, a number of players emerged with credit, among them winger Tom Brown and young centre Chris Dean. But many fans were infuriated by the sidelining of the former Scotland wing Doug Fife, who was released from the club at the end of the season. Fife, the sole try scorer in the 2015 France v Scotland Six Nations match in Paris, however, showed his former Edinburgh paymasters what they had been missing when he scored the winning points in Scotland's dramatic victory over South Africa in the final of the London Sevens at Twickenham.

The criticism levelled at Edinburgh is that too many overseas players are being hired at a time when Scotland desperately needs to give opportunities to home-grown products from the BT Academies. Admittedly, because of the three-year residency rule, 'foreign' players coming to Edinburgh have been useful for the national side, the notable success of this questionable regulation being the

LEFT Glasgow lock Scott Cummings at the centre of a maul against Dragons in the PRO12 fixture at Scotstoun in October 2015.

'tartanisation' of the Afrikaans-speaking WP Nel, now the cornerstone of the Scotland scrum.

Add in back-row Cornell du Preez, who completed his three-year residency period at the start of the 2016-17 season, and the policy at Edinburgh might seem to have some validity. Du Preez has been a class act for Edinburgh in a back row that contains another dynamic player, Hamish Watson. The list of consistent performers in the Edinburgh squad also includes lock Ben Toolis, the hard-working second-row Anton Bresler, prop Rory Sutherland, who was capped last season, and the Scotland Under 20 back-row Jamie Ritchie. Another young success is the Scotland Under 20 full back Blair Kinghorn, who was signed straight from school at the end of the 2015-16 season.

While Edinburgh were well equipped up front, it was their back play that fell short of exhilarating. Part of this was due to the lack of a genuine fly half able to match the skills of Finn Russell at Glasgow. Duncan Weir's move from west to east, however, should address this problem. Some astute observers have suggested that Adam Hastings, the Scotland Under 20 fly half, currently at Bath, should be brought into the Edinburgh team. If he were it would be a special homecoming as Edinburgh are moving to the ground of his old school, George Watson's College, at Myreside at the start of 2017. The well-proportioned Myreside is a sensible alternative to the 67,500-capacity Murrayfield, which has approximately 64,000 more seats than are needed for Edinburgh's average crowd.

Edinburgh's finishing position of ninth in the Guinness PRO12 was very much down to an end-of-season slump that resulted in disheartening defeats to Leinster, Munster and Cardiff Blues that saw Edinburgh fail to make the top six and a place in the Champions Cup. In the European Challenge Cup Edinburgh missed out on the quarter-finals despite finishing level on points in their pool with second-placed London Irish and despite having more wins than the Exiles. But what mattered was the aggregate points difference from the matches played between Edinburgh and London Irish, and it was the Exiles' 38-6 home win that decided the rankings, Edinburgh winning only 18-15 at Murrayfield.

A major problem for player development at both Glasgow and Edinburgh is that neither club plays in a reserve league similar to that which shadows the English Premiership. So what to do with young players who are still on the fringe of playing at professional level? The answer may come from a tie-up between Scottish Rugby and London Scottish, by which young players from north of the border play for the Exiles. Simple though the idea sounds, the negotiations between Murrayfield and the Richmond Athletic Ground were fraught. An initial agreement reached in January 2016 collapsed a few months later with accusations flying in both directions. Then in June, after both sides in the negotiations were brought to their senses, it was back on the agenda, and a done deal, but one significantly scaled down, was announced.

The other route for apprentice and young professional players has been to farm them out to the top-tier amateur clubs. This has, however, not been universally welcomed by the clubs, largely because of the uneven distribution of pro players, an extreme example of which arose when Glasgow Hawks had five 'guests' and Hawick had none. And yes, Hawks won.

There does remain a considerable gulf between amateur and professional club rugby, albeit that the former is improving all the time, helped by better coaching and better conditioning. Retired pro players are now coming into the amateur clubs as coaches and making a difference, as the former Edinburgh centre Ben Cairns showed by guiding Currie RFC to a successful season.

Currie made a challenge both in the league and cup competitions, but it was Heriot's, under the masterful coaching of Phil Smith, who emerged as the outstanding side, winning the league play-offs and achieving the double by securing the Scottish Cup title with victory over Melrose. Smith, voted the amateur coach of the year in Scotland, also piloted the Scotland Club XV to wins over England Counties and Ireland Club XV.

Up until the play-offs, Ayr had been in pole position, but the Millbrae men ultimately lost out to Heriot's. Ayr, however, had another outstanding season and have set the bar high for future competitions. At the other extremity of the BT Premiership, Selkirk, who remain a local club resisting 'buying in' players from elsewhere, were relegated to the second tier, swapping places with the all-conquering and ambitious National League One winners, Watsonians.

As with Glasgow, many amateur clubs were beset by winter flooding, forcing some to consider the installation of plastic pitches. Militating against their introduction, however, is the sheer capital cost, high enough for some to think about an obvious and considerably cheaper alternative. That is to move the game out of the inhospitable Scottish winter and shift the season to a time of year when the weather is seriously conducive to enjoying rugby. It's an issue that divides the rugby community and for many different reasons, but with harmonisation of the global season on the agenda, moving the season in Scotland might just start the oval ball rolling.

Wales: Little Serious Impact
by DAVID STEWART

'At home to Scarlets, Leinster and the Saints had more than 14,000 spectators through the gates. When those teams came to Llanelli, the attendance was halved'

Not so long ago, the measure of a disappointing season was no Welsh region making it through to the knockout stages of the Heineken Cup. The realisation that none made it to the play-offs of the Guinness PRO12 last time around hints at a sobering recalibration of what constitutes success.

Scarlets were, in fifth place, the highest Welsh finishers in the PRO12, ten points behind Leinster and Connacht who contested the play-off final. With Cardiff Blues being the next-highest finisher, in seventh, and only the top six (plus the highest Italian side) qualifying for Europe, the West Wales region will be the only team lining up from the Principality in the next Champions Cup. By way of context, in the early years of professional rugby, they contended to win it – their last-minute semi-final defeat to Leicester in 2002 being a painful memory. Last season, when grouped with Glasgow Warriors, Racing 92 and Northampton Saints, they failed to win a game.

There are of course several reasons for this, some of them mitigating. The wealth of English and especially French clubs, and recent changes in salary caps, have rendered the Celtic teams, but particularly the Welsh ones it seems, comparatively uncompetitive in pursuit of talented players from across the globe. Income derives from several sources: television deals, the union, sponsorship, merchandising and hospitality boxes all play a part, but a glance at crowd figures is instructive. When the Scarlets went to Dublin and Northampton in November, Leinster and the Saints had more than 14,000 spectators through the gates. When those teams came to Llanelli, the attendance was halved.

The first part of last season was affected by the World Cup. The leading teams in the PRO12 all lost significant numbers to the national

RIGHT Hadleigh Parkes crosses for the Scarlets during their 22-12 PRO12 round two home win over Ulster. The Scarlets also won the return in February.

cause. Scarlets seemed to handle it better than most, winning 16-10 in Glasgow, and beating Ulster (22-12), Leinster (25-14) and Munster (25-22) in a run which saw them win their first six games to be league leaders by the time the international players returned at the beginning of November. That momentum did not survive their injury-disrupted European campaign.

That part of next season will be no easier, as their pool includes the might of cup holders Saracens, recent winners Toulon, and Sale Sharks. Reinforcements will be available in the form of centre Jonathan Davies returning from Clermont; Rhys Patchell, who is intended to play fly half, coming from the Blues; Bulls prop Werner Kruger; and back-three player Johnny McNicholl from the Crusaders. Their joining Liam and Scott Williams and Gareth Davies will make for mouth-watering back play, but as ever, it will be the ability of the Scarlets pack to provide sufficient ball which will dictate their chances. That Wales may choose an all-Scarlets front row to start their Autumn Internationals – Rob Evans, Ken Owens and Samson Lee – is an indication of strength.

Like Wayne Pivac in Llanelli, Danny Wilson at the Blues will feel his team made progress, albeit coming from a lower base. For three seasons now, the region have been playing on an artificial 3G pitch. It encourages a fast and exciting style of play, which players and supporters both seemed to be enjoying. Selection has been tailored accordingly. In the latter part of their home fixtures Wilson would employ a back row of three players who are primarily open-side flankers in Sam Warburton (who packed down at blind-side), Josh Navidi (No. 8) and newly capped Ellis Jenkins. With Josh

ABOVE Scarlets-bound Rhys Patchell scores the Blues' fourth try of their 37-28 home win over Munster in the PRO12. The fly half also contributed four conversions and two penalties.

FACING PAGE Scrum half Charlie Davies puts the Dragons through to the semi-finals of the Challenge Cup by touching down in the 76th minute against Gloucester at Kingsholm.

Turnbull, voted player of the season, moving into the second row, it gave the Blues a highly mobile and skilful forward unit.

The Blues started with a big home win against Zebre (61-13), before enduring a horrible run of seven losses in a row, including defeat in Ireland to all four provinces and in the return match in Italy (26-15). That the Arms Park ground was unavailable through its use as a 'fanzone' during the Rugby World Cup was undoubtedly a hindrance, but it meant the capital's team had a run of home fixtures towards the end of the season. This helped them close the campaign with five wins from their last six games, losing only to the Ospreys (40-27) in the highly successful Welsh derby 'double-header' at the Principality Stadium, before a crowd of 68,000.

Their European Challenge Cup pool was a tough one, involving both eventual finalists Montpellier and Harlequins. The Blues can take pride in restricting the winners to 23-22 when they met in France. Their opponents next season include Bath and Bristol, which should do gate receipts no harm at all, and Pau. Newcomers include two Welsh internationals in the exciting utility back Matthew Morgan and prop Rhys Gill, plus former Ulster No. 8 Nick Williams and Hurricanes centre Willis Halaholo. Wilson's overview: 'We have changed the perception slightly. In the latter stages of matches we've played some really good rugby. It proves we are a fit side and we want to maintain that next year.' Gethin Jenkins has been awarded a testimonial year.

It was an odd season for the Ospreys. A talented squad – if one disrupted by RWC more than most – and respected coach in Steve Tandy will have been horrified with five losses from their first seven games, the only wins in that period being over Treviso and Zebre. Once back at full strength in November, their true potential was shown by European Champions Cup wins over Exeter (25-13), Bordeaux-Bègles (19-16) and Clermont Auvergne (21-13). An eighth-place finish in the PRO12 means it will be the Challenge Cup next term, and Lyon, Grenoble and Newcastle rather than some of the more stellar destinations.

Their wonderful leader Alun Wyn Jones will expect players of the quality of Bradley Davies (a significant capture from Wasps), Dan Biggar, Rhys Webb, Scott Baldwin, Dan Lydiate, Justin Tipuric, Eli Walker, Nicky Smith, Dan Baker, Dan Evans and exciting young open-side Sam Underhill (who will be under pressure to return to English rugby) to provide a stronger challenge in 2016-17. An interesting addition is another Crusader in wing/centre Kieron Fonotia.

Times continue to be tough for the Dragons. Another tenth-place finish in the league, with just the Italian teams below them, was bad enough. That the gap to Edinburgh in ninth was as much as 28 points is a stark illustration of how wide the gulf has become. Not for the first time, their future is the subject of debate. Long-standing investor Martyn Hazell is standing down, so attracting new capital is vital. Different business models have been suggested, including becoming a stand-alone region (independent of WRU part-ownership) or continuing as a development region (which some might suggest is the current situation in all but name). The example of Connacht, whose status was similarly lowly not so long ago, should be an inspiration.

The assertion of head coach Kingsley Jones that his squad are 'not far away' is borne out by ten bonus points from matches lost by seven points or less. In a frustrating February, all four league matches were lost, but by two points against Ulster and Treviso, three against Glasgow and five to Connacht. A terrific win (23-21) at Gloucester in the European Challenge Cup quarter-finals was a high point of the season, and the young Dragons players were far from disgraced in going down 22-12 in the away semi-final at powerful Montpellier. The loss of Taulupe Faletau to Bath is a heavy blow, but threequarters Tyler Morgan and Hallam Amos remain to provide a cutting edge behind.

Badly hit by injury, Wales had a World Cup to be proud of, including the famous win over England and running South Africa very close in the quarter-finals. Three wins and a draw made for a reasonable Six Nations Championship. On the tour of New Zealand, a weary squad, at the end of their longest season ever, were competitive in the first two Tests before being heavily beaten in the final one. A painful defeat in the midweek game to a Waikato Chiefs team which was far from full strength was seen as a timely reminder of the gap between the best players in Wales and those a rank below. The struggles of their regional teams to make a serious impact in European and in league competition would seem to reflect that. Supporters of the national team will be fearful that this is indicative of similar times to come, that perhaps Warren Gatland and his coaching team have overachieved since they took over in 2008. Not a happy thought.

Ireland: Clontarf Strike Again

by RUAIDHRI O'CONNOR

'However, the top clubs will be boosted by the union increasing the maximum number of fully contracted professional players allowed in a match-day squad'

For so long, Clontarf were the constant bridesmaids of Ireland's domestic rugby scene. The north Dublin team had heartbreak in their DNA after finishing up as runners-up four times until finally they broke their duck by claiming the league in 2014. After returning to second place a year later, they doubled down on their success in style as Andy Wood brought the title back to Castle Avenue in 2015-16.

The Ulster Bank League often struggles to find a place on the Irish rugby scene so dominated by the professional game, but the televised final grabbed attention as a result of the high quality of rugby played. Standing in 'Tarf's way was a resurgent Cork Constitution side back in league contention for the first time in a number of seasons, attempting to end a run of dominance from the capital city's clubs that has seen the trophy remain in Dublin at the end of every season since 2011.

They came together on a sunny day in May at the Aviva Stadium to decide the honours at the end of a long season and rewarded the small crowd with a high-quality, exciting finale as Leinster Academy out-half Joey Carbery stole the show with a brilliant performance and a 13-point haul. With the teams scoring seven tries between them on a perfect day for rugby, the final was a reminder of what this league can deliver as both teams tore into their task from the off.

Clontarf looked much the stronger team in the first half, racing into a 21-3 lead thanks to tries from Matt D'Arcy, Carbery and Tony Ryan, but Con stormed back after the break and took the game to the wire. Clontarf's 28-25 victory in front of Ireland coach Joe Schmidt consigned memories of last year's defeat to Lansdowne at the same stage to the history books for the Dubliners.

'It was a very tight game. To use a cliché it was a bit of a roller coaster. Credit to Con, they kept coming back at us,' New Zealander Wood said of the final. 'The quality on both sides was evident and thankfully our big players stepped up. To a man, they all performed. There wasn't a lot of reference to last year's game because you don't want to dwell on negatives. We had a lead in that one which didn't come to a good finish. We must like doing it because Con almost caught up with us. It would be easier on the heart if we managed to extend our lead and left the ground running at the start of the second half. Look, that's rugby. Con are an excellent side with super young talents themselves.

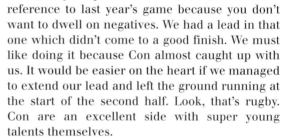

'The fact that we continued to play stood to us in the end. Regardless of the situation and the match points we backed our skills, and took one very important chance in the second half just after they'd scored. We knew Con would come back after half-time. We knew they'd get close. I didn't quite expect them to get that close, if I'm 100 per cent honest. They went after our breakdown on the first two phases and really messed up our momentum on two or three occasions, which got them back into the game. Some of the skills on display from both teams, particularly in our back line, came to the fore. That is literally what got us the result in the end. Some really good work in the first half and then being able to punch it ten minutes into the second half. It was very, very pleasing.'

Clontarf's success was built on a seven-game winning streak at the end of the regular season that saw them top the table and finish as top seeds for the play-offs with an eight-point cushion over Con.

LEFT Clontarf centre Matt D'Arcy touches down for his side's first try of the Ulster Bank League Division 1A final at the Aviva Stadium. 'Tarf won the match 28-25.

Early on in the campaign, the clubs found themselves stretched as a result of the Rugby World Cup, which put a strain on provincial squads and afforded opportunities for club players to make their mark in the professional game. Despite a hefty contingent at Leinster, University College Dublin (UCD) were the early frontrunners in the league campaign and reached the play-offs for the first time by finishing fourth, while Young Munster returned to the final four with a strong showing. They ran Con close in their semi-final despite having to travel to Temple Hill, but UCD struggled to get near Clontarf in their knockout clash and a memorable season came to an end at Castle Avenue.

There was some consolation for Cork Constitution who continued their complete dominance in the cup competitions as they secured the Bateman (All Ireland) Cup for the fourth successive season in comprehensive fashion. The cup kings proved too strong for Connacht champions Galwegians at Crowley Park in late April, running in four tries in a 38-19 win over the westerners, with Ryan Foley crossing twice to secure an historic triumph.

Although they couldn't finish the job in the league, it was a memorable season for Brian Hickey's men. 'It was an unreal team to be involved in. We had a successful season. If you'd offered me the season we've had in September I'd have taken it and been happy with it,' the Ulster Bank Division 1A Player of the Year Conor Kindregan of Cork Con said.

'The disappointment of the league final was hard to take after we worked so hard to get there, to earn a home semi-final but it has been a good season. The Munster Senior Cup and the Bateman Cup were my first two cups, it's the four-in-a-row for the club and it was great to be involved in it.'

It was a disappointing season for the club they had overcome in the final as Galwegians were relegated automatically after finishing bottom of the Division 1A table. Their demotion, along with Ballynahinch, meant that Connacht and Ulster will have no representation in the top flight this season after the two strugglers claimed just five wins each in their 18 games.

The western side will be replaced by St Mary's who return to Division 1A at the first attempt, while Dublin University are back in the big time after they beat Ballynahinch 18-9 away from home in their play-off game to secure promotion. It means that this year's league has a distinctly metropolitan feel to it, with seven Dublin clubs being joined by Limerick's Garryowen and Young Munster, and Con, who are Cork's representatives.

St Mary's, who won Division 1A in 2012 but were relegated three years later, swiftly returned to the top table with 16 wins out of 18 over the course of a dominant campaign. They finished two points clear of Dublin University at the top of Division 1B, with third-placed Ballymena a further 16 points back.

Naas topped Division 2A ahead of Banbridge and both sides will play in Division 1B next season, with Blackrock College and Belfast Harlequins relegated, while Cork sides Highfield, who topped the table, and Sundays Well were promoted from Division 2B at the expense of Skerries and Thomond. Old Crescent claimed the Division 2C title and were promoted with Wanderers, who won the play-off.

The Ireland Club XV came together in February and secured an away win over France Fédérale for the first time thanks to Ballymena man Connor Smyth's charge-down try that secured a 16-12 win in Massy. However, Paul Cunningham's side couldn't back up that result a few weeks later when they hosted Scotland Club XV at Temple Hill, with the visitors emerging as 19-13 winners despite tries from Mark Roche and Daniel Riordan.

At the end of the season, the IRFU concluded that the current format of five divisions consisting of ten teams would remain until the end of the 2017-18 season at least after consulting with a range of clubs and stakeholders. However, the top clubs will be boosted by the union increasing the maximum number of fully contracted professional players allowed in a match-day squad from two to four, of which two can be forwards, in a move designed to increase the intensity and quality of the games and the players involved.

Certainly, league-winning coach Wood believes that the competition is moving in the right direction. 'I think the league is in good health. I've thought that for a number of years now,' the Clontarf supremo said. 'I've seen, not just from ourselves but across the board, coaches and players who have put in huge amounts of effort and the quality that's coming out of it individually and across clubs can only be good for Irish rugby. It's great to see.'

France: Good News and Bad News

by CHRIS THAU

'The final itself was the dream encounter, in a dream venue, as the league decided to book Camp Nou, the monumental FC Barcelona home ground of 99,354 seats, for the match'

As usual, there is good news and bad news from France. Significantly the good news is on the playing front, as the new France head coach, Guy Novès, true to his track record, has been turning things around pretty fast since his appointment. After a modest Six Nations Championship, during which France blew hot and cold – winning two (by two points and one point respectively against Italy and Ireland) and losing three (to Scotland, England and Wales) – the new French team have offered a fascinating glimpse of their potential during the eventful tour of Argentina in June, when after losing the first Test 30-19, they won the second 27-0, after a performance described by both friend and foe as 'stirring'.

After 'the luckiest Six Nations in living memory', as one scribe put it, very few among the normally assertive French media seemed prepared to point a finger at Novès. They mumbled and grumbled, but deferred judgment, understanding the difficulty faced by the head coach in rebuilding the team. The humiliating 62-13 demolition at the hands of the All Blacks in the RWC 2015 quarter-finals the previous autumn had bought the former Toulouse supremo a valuable breathing space, which he and his coaching staff of Yannick Bru and Jeff Dubois used cleverly. During the Six Nations they either searched for new talent, or experimented with old campaigners in new positions. They carried on with the renewal programme into the summer tour, implicitly helped by the absence of about a dozen of France's leading internationals, unavailable due to championship semi-finals business.

Without the players from Montpellier, Toulon, Racing 92 and Clermont, Novès had to dig much deeper for talent and what he has found must have pleased him no end. France left for Buenos Aires with probably the most inexperienced squad in history, but Novès kept his proverbial cool. Though 12 of the 28 tourists were uncapped, with the first Test line-up in Tucumán featuring seven newcomers among the starters alone, he reminded the players that it was business as usual and that wearing the blue, white or red jersey of France was the pinnacle of one's sporting career. Old-fashioned, perhaps, but true and for his young players, effective. Luckily, Novès' former club Toulouse had been knocked out in the championship play-offs, so he had access to five quality regulars (his former players) for what was expected and proved to be a testing, yet confusing, series.

At the end of the tour, several newcomers made strong claims to a regular place in the French starting XV, with Bordeaux-Bègles scrum half Baptiste Serin, Castres Olympique centre Rémi Lamerat, winger Hugo Bonneval of Stade Français, Brive-bound forward Julien Le Devedec and back-row Kevin Gourdon of La Rochelle particularly impressive. Add to that the erratic genius of François Trinh-Duc, snubbed by previous administrations, who had a cracking tour, and one could understand why Novès declared himself cautiously satisfied with the outcome.

'There was clear progress after the Six Nations, as an increasingly large number of players have understood and subscribed to the new playing approach. I felt we were in the mix as far as the northern hemisphere were concerned, but I am not sure that this is valid for the nations of the south. As far as the Argentina we encountered are concerned, I do not believe they are at the level of New Zealand, Australia or South Africa ... We will find out more in the autumn ... I am not prepared to judge the team based on the 27-0 win in the second Test; it would show lack of humility. I must take into account the defeat in the first Test, the fact that we were in the lead after 60 minutes and the way our defence collapsed, as the Pumas cut through it like it was a piece of butter. It was too bad to be true ... But again, overall, in terms of our new approach, we made progress,' Novès said after the tour. The November Test series against Samoa, Australia and New Zealand will most certainly enable him to further integrate the uncut diamonds unearthed during the Argentina trip, with the rest of the assets left behind, into what he describes as the 'new approach'.

Meanwhile, in the first of the French Championship semi-finals, played during the French tour, the red 'mean machine' of Toulon, with their Welsh full back Leigh Halfpenny in imperious form after a long and frustrating injury break, put the Montpellier juggernaut to the sword 27-18. In the other semi-final, an increasingly confident Racing 92, after their defeat of Toulouse in the play-offs, had literally managed to sneak in at the close, defeating Clermont 34-33 thanks to Juan Imhoff's late – very, very late – try, in injury time, followed by Carter's charmed conversion.

The final itself was the dream encounter, in a dream venue, as the league decided to book Camp Nou, the monumental FC Barcelona home ground of 99,354 seats, for the match. The grand occasion, nearly ruined by referee Mathieu Raynal who sent off Racing playmaker Maxime Machenaud after 20 minutes for an awkward tackle on Matt Giteau, survived the shock, due to Imhoff's unique ability to seamlessly morph himself into Machenaud's role, as well as the mesmeric effect Daniel Carter's presence in the Racing ranks has had on both team-mates and opponents. He simply could not put a foot wrong, inspiring the former and overwhelming the latter. If the retired Jonny Wilkinson was the hero of the 2014 final, this one, despite Imhoff's fairy tale, was Carter's as he employed his sublime skills and cheerful confidence in Racing's 29-21 victory.

A final acknowledgement for the Racing 92 coaching duo Laurent Travers and Laurent Labit, who after success with Castres Olympique

BELOW Former France hooker and captain Raphaël Ibanez, with broadcasting colleague, soaks up the atmosphere of Barcelona's Camp Nou ground ahead of the 2016 Top 14 final.

in 2013 won their second Bouclier de Brennus in three years, and commiserations for their defeated Toulon counterpart Bernard Laporte, who after five seasons and four championship finals (plus three European Cup wins) departed for pastures new.

And now the bad news! After all that, the civil war is about to start, or has already started, in French rugby, if one reads the front page of the weekly *Midi Olympique*, which announced at the beginning of July '*C'est la guerre!*' And surprise, surprise, Bernard Laporte, whose political ambitions always blended with his coaching career – he became French Sports Minister under President Sarkozy – is one of the protagonists. Long before the championship final Laporte had announced that he was going to challenge the incumbent FFR president, Pierre Camou, for the top position in French rugby. Supported by several club presidents, including his former boss Mourad Boudjellal of Toulon, Laporte has made his renewal programme public, which has generated an unusual and probably healthy level of debate within French rugby.

It is quite clear that the call for transparency of the former Toulon and France coach has touched a nerve within the normally sedated French rugby set-up, increasingly hassled by the conflicting demands of the elite clubs and its huge amateur structure on the one hand and a dated management structure on the other, not to mention what the French call 'the Grand Stadium project', the construction of the FFR's own mega-stadium. To add to the drama that unfolded during the 140th Congress in the summer, the FFR general secretary, Alain Doucet, announced that he might just as well decide to stand for the presidency, which further complicated the matter. A survey among 57 of the club presidents attending the Pau Congress revealed that the support for Camou (43.9 per cent) was just below the combined vote for Laporte and Doucet (45.6).

Italy: A New Regime

by CHRIS THAU

'The Championship final was a fairly balanced affair, with man of the match full back Stefan Basson making the difference with his accurate kicking'

The three-Test Italian tour in the summer could be described as an audacious yet pragmatic foray into the future by new head coach Conor O'Shea. Two wins by a score or less against nominally second-tier powers and a defeat by six points at the hands of the Pumas should be viewed as a promising return by the former Harlequins supremo, though by top international standards the margins in the three Tests suggest modest progress, rather than massive advancement. The truth is that there is no other way to make progress in Italian rugby other than by employing the policy of small steps.

O'Shea knows Italian rugby well from his days as a dashing full back for Ireland in the 1990s, when Italy were painstakingly making the case for inclusion among the then Five Nations. He must have impressed his prospective employers with his enthusiasm and hard-nosed expertise, as well as his plans to transform *Squadra Azzurra* into 'best ever Italian team'. Technically and tactically, his predecessor Jacques Brunel has taken Italy to another level, but, as O'Shea has correctly identified, the fitness and the mindset of the Italian team are key to further progress. Unquestionably, the tour to Argentina, the USA and Canada has proved

BELOW Ornel Gega goes over against the USA in San Jose, California, as Italy register their first victory of Conor O'Shea's tenure as national head coach. The hooker scored both of Italy's tries in the match.

a success in more than one way, as his young recruits have risen to the occasion, though a number of questions remain unanswered.

Overall, there is good news, as assistant coach Mike Catt observed halfway through the tour. 'The boys have trust in the defensive system we employ and are genuinely proud to play for their country, which is very important. There is a lot of positive energy in this squad and the quality of our work keeps improving from one match to the next,' Catt said.

Conspicuous through his absence on tour was emblematic captain Sergio Parisse, replaced as skipper for the three-Test summer series by the increasingly influential scrum half Edoardo Gori, who added three more caps to his half a century pre-tour tally. Parisse is one of the few world-class players in the Italian set-up and at 32 he needs as much rest as possible to enable him to recharge his batteries. Likewise, his back-row partners Alessandro Zanni and Francesco Minto have been given time off by O'Shea, but I expect them to be available for selection in the autumn. Two of the original tour back-row novices Andries van Schalkwyk (two caps pre-tour) and Maxime Mbandà (uncapped) have confirmed their potential, though the third, Abraham Steyn (three caps), got injured and was replaced after only ten minutes against Argentina. This brought the 22-year-old Hartpury College hopeful Sebastian Negri into contention – from the Emerging Italy team playing in the World Rugby Nations Cup in Bucharest – though he may have to wait a while to add a third cap to those he won against the USA and Canada.

BELOW Femi-CZ Rugby Rovigo Delta celebrate their first Italian Championship in 26 years after defeating Calvisano 20-13 in the final of the Campionato d'Eccellenza at Rovigo.

The front row, one of the traditional assets of the Italian team, has been given an overhaul, with veterans Leonardo Ghiraldini and Martin

CAMPIONE D'ITALIA
2015 - 2016

Castrogiovanni left behind to rest, though Castrogiovanni's antics in Las Vegas in the spring are unlikely to have impressed O'Shea. The eight front-rowers selected at the beginning of the tour shared between them 67 caps, 47 of which belonged to Wasps' Lorenzo Cittadini, the most senior front-row citizen on tour, who is joining Bayonne for 2016-17. Among the props, two newcomers, Sami Panico and Simone Ferrari, as well as Pietro Ceccarelli (one cap) and Andrea Lovotti (five caps) have done a fair deal both in Argentina and North America to enhance their status. Meanwhile among the three hookers originally selected – Ornel Gega (two caps), Oliviero Fabiani (two caps) and Tommaso d'Apice (ten caps) – Gega of Treviso, who scored three tries on tour, must have definitely moved ahead in the pecking order for that position.

The Italian cupboard is not at all empty, as proven by the gallant performance of Emerging Italy in the WR Nations Cup in Bucharest in June. Coached by former Italy hooker Carlo Orlandi, the young Italians gave a good account of themselves, but both their fitness and mental strength need to be looked at, as Emerging Italy are likely to be increasingly used by O'Shea to enlarge his recruitment base. During the senior tour, David Odiete, Treviso-bound from the Mogliano club, added another three appearances to his four-cap tally, while centres Tommaso Castello and Tommaso Boni made their international debuts.

Outside half Carlo Canna appeared in all three Tests, but yellow cards in the last two matches suggest that discipline not talent is his main shortcoming. After the USA Test, the first win of the O'Shea reign, the Irishman gave the players credit for a well-earned victory despite being exhausted after a 30-hour trip from Santa Fe in Argentina to San Jose in the US. 'I am happy for the boys and the way they overcame the difficult moments and won. It was a very long, exhausting trip from Santa Fe for this very young team, so I am quite pleased the way they kept on playing aggressively until the end, as I asked them to do,' he said.

Though time is not on O'Shea's side, the November series and the 2017 Six Nations will provide him with more intelligence on the genuine potential of the new-look Italy.

Due to some FIR administrative oversight his appointment is out of sync with his French and English counterparts, Guy Novès and Eddie Jones respectively, who commenced their period in office nearly one year earlier. This could be a distinct handicap for the Italians in the build-up to RWC 2019, though it might well act as an incentive for O'Shea and his assistant Mike Catt to speed up the process during the 2017 Six Nations.

Meanwhile, Femi-CZ Rovigo, led by their South African-born hooker Jacques Momberg and coached by Joe McDonnell, beat Rugby Calvisano 20-13 in the final of the eighty-sixth Italian Championship, their first national title since 1990. In the semi-final play-offs Rovigo defeated Mogliano 13-10 and 34-17, while Calvisano qualified at the expense of Petrarca of Padua, whom they defeated 11-3 and 33-7.

The final, played at the Mario Battaglini Stadium in Rovigo on 28 May, was a fairly balanced affair, with man of the match full back Stefan Basson making the difference with his accurate kicking. In the first half Basson landed two penalties to Calvisano's one dropped goal and one penalty, signed off by their new fly half Florin Vlaicu. In the second half, both Rovigo's Ross McCann and Alesio Zdrilich of Calvisano scored tries, but while Vlaicu was on target with one conversion only, Basson landed three more penalties to secure Rovigo the coveted title.

A Summary of the Season 2015-16

by TERRY COOPER

RUGBY WORLD CUP 2015

POOL A

England	35	Fiji	11
Wales	54	Uruguay	9
Australia	28	Fiji	13
England	25	Wales	28
Australia	65	Uruguay	3
Wales	23	Fiji	13
England	13	Australia	33
Fiji	47	Uruguay	15
Australia	15	Wales	6
England	60	Uruguay	3

	P	W	D	L	F	A	BP	Pts
Australia	4	4	0	0	141	35	1	17
Wales	4	3	0	1	111	62	1	13
England	4	2	0	2	133	75	3	11
Fiji	4	1	0	3	84	101	1	5
Uruguay	4	0	0	4	30	226	0	0

POOL B

South Africa	32	Japan	34
Samoa	25	USA	16
Scotland	45	Japan	10
South Africa	46	Samoa	6
Scotland	39	USA	16
Samoa	5	Japan	26
South Africa	34	Scotland	16
South Africa	64	USA	0
Samoa	33	Scotland	36
USA	18	Japan	28

	P	W	D	L	F	A	BP	Pts
South Africa	4	3	0	1	176	56	4	16
Scotland	4	3	0	1	136	93	2	14
Japan	4	3	0	1	98	100	0	12
Samoa	4	1	0	3	69	124	2	6
USA	4	0	0	4	50	156	0	0

POOL C

Tonga	10	Georgia	17
New Zealand	26	Argentina	16
New Zealand	58	Namibia	14
Argentina	54	Georgia	9
Tonga	35	Namibia	21
New Zealand	43	Georgia	10
Argentina	45	Tonga	16
Namibia	16	Georgia	17
New Zealand	47	Tonga	9
Argentina	64	Namibia	19

	P	W	D	L	F	A	BP	Pts
New Zealand	4	4	0	0	174	49	3	19
Argentina	4	3	0	1	179	70	3	15
Georgia	4	2	0	2	53	123	0	8
Tonga	4	1	0	3	70	130	2	6
Namibia	4	0	0	4	70	174	1	1

POOL D

Ireland	50	Canada	7
France	32	Italy	10
France	38	Romania	11
Italy	23	Canada	18
Ireland	44	Romania	10
France	41	Canada	18
Ireland	16	Italy	9
Canada	15	Romania	17
Italy	32	Romania	22
France	9	Ireland	24

	P	W	D	L	F	A	BP	Pts
Ireland	4	4	0	0	134	35	2	18
France	4	3	0	1	120	63	2	14
Italy	4	2	0	2	74	88	2	10
Romania	4	1	0	3	60	129	0	4
Canada	4	0	0	4	58	131	2	2

KNOCKOUT STAGES

Quarter-finals

South Africa	23	Wales	19
New Zealand	62	France	13
Ireland	20	Argentina	43
Australia	35	Scotland	34

Semi-finals

South Africa	18	New Zealand	20
Argentina	15	Australia	29

Bronze Final

South Africa	24	Argentina	13

Final

New Zealand	34	Australia	17

INTERNATIONAL RUGBY

ENGLAND TO AUSTRALIA, JUNE 2016

Opponents	Results
AUSTRALIA	W 39-28
AUSTRALIA	W 23-7
AUSTRALIA	W 44-40
Played 3 Won 3	

SCOTLAND TO JAPAN, JUNE 2016

Opponents	Results
JAPAN	W 26-13
JAPAN	W 21-16
Played 2 Won 2	

WALES TO NEW ZEALAND, JUNE 2016

Opponents	Results
NEW ZEALAND	L 21-39
Chiefs	L 7-40
NEW ZEALAND	L 22-36
NEW ZEALAND	L 6-46
Played 4 Lost 4	

IRELAND TO SOUTH AFRICA, JUNE 2016

Opponents	Results
SOUTH AFRICA	W 26-20
SOUTH AFRICA	L 26-32
SOUTH AFRICA	L 13-19
Played 3 Won 1 Lost 2	

FRANCE TO ARGENTINA, JUNE 2016

Opponents	Results
ARGENTINA	L 19-30
ARGENTINA	W 27-0
Played 2 Won 1 Lost 1	

ITALY TO THE AMERICAS, JUNE 2016

Opponents	Results
ARGENTINA	L 24-30
USA	W 24-20
CANADA	W 20-18
Played 3 Won 2 Lost 1	

ENGLAND SAXONS TO SOUTH AFRICA, JUNE 2016

Opponents	Results
South Africa A	W 32-24
South Africa A	W 29-26
Played 2 Won 2	

RBS 6 NATIONS CHAMPIONSHIP 2016

France	23	Italy	21
Scotland	9	England	15
Ireland	16	Wales	16
France	10	Ireland	9
Wales	27	Scotland	23
Italy	9	England	40
Wales	19	France	10
Italy	20	Scotland	36
England	21	Ireland	10
Ireland	58	Italy	15
England	25	Wales	21
Scotland	29	France	18
Wales	67	Italy	14
Ireland	35	Scotland	25
France	21	England	31

	P	W	D	L	F	A	PD	Pts
England	5	5	0	0	132	70	62	10
Wales	5	3	1	1	150	88	62	7
Ireland	5	2	1	2	128	87	41	5
Scotland	5	2	0	3	122	115	7	4
France	5	2	0	3	82	109	-27	4
Italy	5	0	0	5	79	224	-145	0

WOMEN'S SIX NATIONS 2016

Scotland	0	England	32
Ireland	21	Wales	3
France	39	Italy	0
Italy	24	England	33
France	18	Ireland	6
Wales	23	Scotland	10
England	13	Ireland	9
Wales	10	France	8
Italy	22	Scotland	7
Scotland	0	France	24
England	20	Wales	13
Ireland	14	Italy	3
France	17	England	12
Ireland	45	Scotland	12
Wales	12	Italy	16

	P	W	D	L	F	A	PD	Pts
France	5	4	0	1	106	28	78	8
England	5	4	0	1	110	63	47	8
Ireland	5	3	0	2	95	49	46	6
Wales	5	2	0	3	61	75	-14	4
Italy	5	2	0	3	65	105	-40	4
Scotland	5	0	0	5	29	146	-117	0

UNDER 20 SIX NATIONS 2016

Ireland	24	Wales	35
Scotland	24	England	6
France	40	Italy	3
Wales	18	Scotland	15
Italy	7	England	42
France	34	Ireland	13
England	20	Ireland	26
Italy	14	Scotland	24
Wales	16	France	10
Ireland	19	Italy	13

England	16	Wales	42
Scotland	21	France	36
France	41	England	17
Wales	35	Italy	6
Ireland	26	Scotland	18

	P	W	D	L	F	A	PD	Pts
Wales	5	5	0	0	146	71	75	10
France	5	4	0	1	161	70	91	8
Ireland	5	3	0	2	108	120	-12	6
Scotland	5	2	0	3	102	100	2	4
England	5	1	0	4	101	140	-39	2
Italy	5	0	0	5	43	160	-117	0

WORLD RUGBY PACIFIC NATIONS CUP 2016

(Held in June in Suva and Apia)

Fiji	23	Tonga	18
Fiji	26	Samoa	16
Samoa	30	Tonga	10

Champions: Fiji

WORLD RUGBY NATIONS CUP 2016

(Held in June in Bucharest)

Argentina XV	44	Spain	8
Uruguay	24	Emerging Italy	26
Namibia	8	Romania	20
Argentina XV	40	Emerging Italy	30
Namibia	34	Spain	32
Uruguay	0	Romania	40
Uruguay	16	Spain	0
Namibia	38	Emerging Italy	26
Argentina XV	8	Romania	20

Champions: Romania

WORLD RUGBY U20 CHAMPIONSHIP 2016

(Held in June in Manchester)

Final
| Ireland | 21 | England | 45 |

WORLD RUGBY U20 TROPHY 2016

(Held in April/May in Harare)

Final
| Samoa | 38 | Spain | 32 |

OTHER INTERNATIONAL MATCH 2016

| England | 27 | Wales | 13 |

WORLD CUP WARM-UP MATCHES 2015

| Wales | 21 | Ireland | 35 |
| New Zealand | 41 | Australia | 13 |

(also Bledisloe Cup)

England	19	France	14
Argentina	12	South Africa	26
Ireland	28	Scotland	22
France	25	England	20
Italy	12	Scotland	16
Ireland	10	Wales	16
Scotland	48	Italy	7
England	21	Ireland	13
Wales	23	Italy	19
France	19	Scotland	16
USA	10	Australia	47

THE RUGBY CHAMPIONSHIP 2015

New Zealand	39	Argentina	18
Australia	24	South Africa	20
South Africa	20	New Zealand	27
Argentina	9	Australia	34
Australia	27	New Zealand	19

(also Bledisloe Cup)

| South Africa | 25 | Argentina | 37 |

	P	W	D	L	PD	BP	Pts
Australia	3	3	0	0	37	1	13
New Zealand	3	2	0	1	20	1	9
Argentina	3	1	0	2	-34	1	5
South Africa	3	0	0	3	-23	2	2

Champions: Australia
(Condensed championship because of RWC)

HSBC WORLD RUGBY SEVENS SERIES FINALS 2015-16

Dubai
| Fiji | 28 | England | 17 |

South Africa (Cape Town)
| South Africa | 29 | Argentina | 14 |

New Zealand (Wellington)
| New Zealand | 24 | South Africa | 21 |

Australia (Sydney)
| New Zealand | 27 | Australia | 24 |

USA (Las Vegas)
| Fiji | 21 | Australia | 15 |

Canada (Vancouver)
| South Africa | 14 | New Zealand | 19 |

Hong Kong
| New Zealand | 7 | Fiji | 21 |

Singapore
| Fiji | 7 | Kenya | 30 |

France (Paris)
| Samoa | 29 | Fiji | 26 |

England (Twickenham)
| South Africa | 26 | Scotland | 27 |

Champions: Fiji

HSBC WORLD RUGBY WOMEN'S SEVENS SERIES FINALS 2015-16

Dubai
| Russia | 12 | Australia | 31 |

Brazil (São Paulo)
| Australia | 29 | Canada | 0 |

USA (Atlanta)
| New Zealand | 19 | Australia | 24 |

Canada (Langford)
| England | 31 | New Zealand | 14 |

France (Clermont-Ferrand)
| Canada | 29 | Australia | 19 |

Champions: Australia

2016 OLYMPIC RUGBY SEVENS

MEN'S COMPETITION

POOL A

	P	W	D	L	PD	Pts
Fiji	3	3	0	0	40	9
Argentina	3	2	0	1	27	7
USA	3	1	0	2	18	5
Brazil	3	0	0	3	-85	3

POOL B

	P	W	D	L	PD	Pts
South Africa	3	2	0	1	43	7
France	3	2	0	1	12	7
Australia	3	2	0	1	4	7
Spain	3	0	0	3	-59	3

POOL C

	P	W	D	L	PD	Pts
Great Britain	3	3	0	0	28	9
Japan	3	2	0	1	24	7
New Zealand	3	1	0	2	19	5
Kenya	3	0	0	3	-71	3

Ninth- to Twelfth-place Play-offs
USA	24	Brazil	12
Spain	14	Kenya	12

Eleventh-place Match
Brazil	0	Kenya	24

Ninth-place Match
USA	24	Spain	12

Quarter-finals
Fiji	12	New Zealand	7
Japan	12	France	7
Great Britain	5	Argentina	0
South Africa	22	Australia	5

Fifth- to Eighth-place Play-offs
New Zealand	24	France	19
Argentina	26	Australia	21

Seventh-place Match
France	12	Australia	10

Fifth-place Match
New Zealand	17	Argentina	14

Semi-finals
Fiji	20	Japan	5
Great Britain	7	South Africa	5

Bronze Medal Match
Japan	14	South Africa	54

Gold Medal Match
Fiji	43	Great Britain	7

WOMEN'S COMPETITION

POOL A

	P	W	D	L	PD	Pts
Australia	3	2	1	0	89	8
Fiji	3	2	0	1	5	7
USA	3	1	1	1	43	6
Colombia	3	0	0	3	-137	3

POOL B

	P	W	D	L	PD	Pts
New Zealand	3	3	0	0	97	9
France	3	2	0	1	31	7
Spain	3	1	0	2	-34	5
Kenya	3	0	0	3	-94	3

POOL C

	P	W	D	L	PD	Pts
Great Britain	3	3	0	0	88	9
Canada	3	2	0	1	61	7
Brazil	3	1	0	2	-48	5
Japan	3	0	0	3	-101	3

Ninth- to Twelfth-place Play-offs
Brazil	24	Colombia	0
Japan	24	Kenya	0

Eleventh-place Match
Colombia	10	Kenya	22

Ninth-place Match
Brazil	33	Japan	5

Quarter-finals
Australia	24	Spain	0
Canada	15	France	5
Great Britain	26	Fiji	7
New Zealand	5	USA	0

Fifth- to Eighth-place Play-offs
Spain	12	France	24
Fiji	7	USA	12

Seventh-place Match
Spain	21	Fiji	0

Fifth-place Match
France	5	USA	19

Semi-finals
Australia	17	Canada	5
Great Britain	7	New Zealand	25

Bronze Medal Match
Canada	33	Great Britain	10

Gold Medal Match
Australia	24	New Zealand	17

CLUB, COUNTY AND DIVISIONAL RUGBY

ENGLAND

Aviva Premiership

	P	W	D	L	F	A	BP	Pts
Saracens	22	17	1	4	580	376	10	80
Exeter	22	15	0	7	585	361	14	74
Wasps	22	15	0	7	598	397	12	72
Leicester	22	14	0	8	509	475	9	65
Northampton	22	12	0	10	455	392	12	60
Sale	22	11	2	9	456	459	10	58
Harlequins	22	10	1	11	547	583	13	55
Gloucester	22	10	1	11	429	423	7	49
Bath	22	9	0	13	435	460	12	48
Worcester	22	7	0	15	420	597	7	35
Newcastle	22	5	1	16	357	556	5	27
London Irish	22	4	0	18	328	620	4	20

Relegated: London Irish

Aviva Premiership Play-offs
Semi-finals
Saracens	44	Leicester	17
Exeter	34	Wasps	23

Final
Saracens	28	Exeter	20

Greene King IPA Championship Play-offs
Semi-finals (1st leg)
Bedford	16	Bristol	45
Yorkshire Carnegie	17	Doncaster Knights	30

Semi-finals (2nd leg)
Bristol	45	Bedford	19
Doncaster Knights	14	Yorkshire Carnegie	17

Final
Doncaster Knights	13	Bristol	28
Bristol	32	Doncaster Knights	34

Promoted to Premiership: Bristol

National Leagues
National 1 Champions: Richmond
Runners-up: Hartpury College
National 2 (S) Champions: Cambridge
Runners-up: Old Albanians
National 2 (N) Champions: Macclesfield
Runners-up: Sedgley Park

National 2 N & S Runners-up Play-off
Old Albanians	24	Sedgley Park	0

RFU Knockout Trophies Finals
Intermediate Cup
St Benedicts	14	Tunbridge Wells	56

Senior Vase
West Leeds	42	Withycombe	22

Junior Vase
Buxton	0	Old Cranleighans	50

County Championships
Bill Beaumont Cup Division 1 Final
Cheshire	13	Cornwall	35

Bill Beaumont Cup Division 2 (Plate) Final
East Midlands	33	Kent	27

County Championship Shield Final
Hampshire	33	Staffordshire	11

National U20 Championship Final
Yorkshire	53	Northumberland	20

National Under 17 Cup Final
York	13	Worthing	18

Oxbridge University Matches
Varsity Match
Oxford	12	Cambridge	6

Women's Varsity Match
Oxford	0	Cambridge	52

BUCS Competitions
Men's Championship Winners: Exeter University
Women's Championship Winners: Cardiff Met

Inter-Services Championship
Royal Navy	9	Royal Air Force	8
Royal Air Force	13	Army	12
Army	29	Royal Navy	29

Champions: Royal Navy

Hospitals Cup Winners: St George's

Rosslyn Park HSBC National Schools Sevens
Cup Winners: Cranleigh
Vase Winners: Tonbridge
Girls Winners: Amman Valley School
Girls AASE Winners: Hartpury College
Colts Winners: Brighton College
U14 Winners: Ivybridge Community College
Junior Winners: Wimbledon College
Prep Winners: Caldicott

NatWest Schools Cup Finals Day
Under 18 Cup Winners: Bromsgrove
Under 18 Vase Winners: Northampton SFB
Under 15 Cup Winners: Sedbergh School
Under 15 Vase Winners: Dr Challoner's GS

Women's Premiership

	P	W	D	L	F	A	BP	Pts
Richmond	14	13	0	1	531	139	11	63
Saracens	14	13	0	1	502	139	9	61
Lichfield	14	8	0	6	476	255	11	43
Worcester	14	8	0	6	418	260	9	41
Bristol	14	8	0	6	392	271	8	40
Wasps	14	4	0	10	240	469	3	19
Darlington MP	14	1	0	13	210	512	6	10
Aylesford Bulls	14	1	0	13	73	797	0	4

SCOTLAND

BT Cup Final
Melrose	13	Heriot's	21

BT Shield Final
Highland	27	Carrick	34

BT Bowl Final
Millbrae	17	Aberdeen U	15

Scottish Sevens Winners
Gala: Watsonians
Melrose: Edinburgh
Hawick: Hawick
Berwick: Jed-Forest
Langholm: Watsonians
Peebles: Selkirk
Kelso: Melrose
Earlston: Jed-Forest
Selkirk: Melrose
Jed-Forest: Jed-Forest
Kings of the Sevens: Jed-Forest

BT Premiership
	P	W	D	L	F	A	BP	Pts
Ayr	18	14	0	4	538	298	12	68
Currie	18	12	1	5	445	338	9	59
Heriot's	18	11	1	6	428	305	10	56
Melrose	18	11	1	6	399	348	8	54
Boroughmuir	18	9	1	8	392	372	8	46
Glasgow Hawks	18	9	0	9	353	325	9	45
Hawick	18	9	0	9	361	382	7	43
Stirling County	18	6	1	11	361	443	9	35
Gala	18	5	1	12	375	442	10	32
Selkirk	18	1	0	17	287	686	5	9

BT Premiership Play-off Final
Ayr	26	Heriot's	29

BT National League Division 1
	P	W	D	L	F	A	BP	Pts
Watsonians	22	17	0	5	786	468	22	90
Marr	22	18	0	4	636	445	12	84
Dundee HSFP	22	16	1	5	687	406	17	83
Jed-Forest	22	14	0	8	561	491	14	70
Edinburgh Acads	22	13	1	8	585	414	14	68
Stewart's Melville	22	9	0	13	468	521	11	47
GHA	22	8	0	14	528	648	11	43
Musselburgh	22	8	1	13	538	702	9	43
Aberdeen GS	22	8	0	14	561	630	10	42
Howe of Fife	22	7	1	14	434	585	11	41
Peebles	22	6	0	16	409	594	11	35
Kelso	22	4	4	14	415	704	6	30

BT Premiership-National 1 Play-off
Marr	10	Gala	22

BT Women's Premier League
Champions: Murrayfield Wanderers

Sarah Beaney Cup
Winners: Murrayfield Wanderers

WALES

National Cup Final
Carmarthen Quins	18	Llandovery	25

National Plate Final
Bedlinog	12	Penallta	10

National Bowl Final
Burry Port	20	Taffs Well	18

Principality Premiership
	P	W	D	L	F	A	BP	Pts
Pontypridd	22	17	0	5	678	434	13	81
Llandovery	22	15	0	7	644	374	17	77
Ebbw Vale	22	16	0	6	508	394	10	74
Cross Keys	22	15	1	6	600	468	11	73
Aberavon	22	13	2	7	544	428	14	70
Newport	22	12	0	10	608	556	19	67
Bedwas	22	10	0	12	562	550	16	56
Llanelli	22	10	0	12	632	650	12	52
Cardiff Rugby	22	8	0	14	492	676	11	43
Bridgend	22	7	0	15	338	628	6	34
C'marthen Quins	22	6	0	16	464	580	10	34
Neath	22	1	1	20	386	718	10	16

National Championship
	P	W	D	L	F	A	BP	Pts
Merthyr	26	24	0	2	1192	289	22	118
Swansea	26	22	1	3	859	402	18	108
Bargoed	26	19	1	6	779	401	19	97
RGC 1404	26	19	0	7	928	460	20	96
Pontypool	26	19	1	6	794	428	16	94
Beddau	26	10	1	15	537	567	10	52
Cardiff Met	26	9	0	17	631	828	15	51
Tata Steel	26	11	0	15	622	787	14	50
Narberth	26	8	1	17	564	710	14	48
Newcastle Emlyn	26	10	0	16	538	668	7	47
Newbridge	26	9	0	17	501	686	11	47
Glynneath	26	9	0	17	461	767	9	45
Bridgend Ath	26	9	1	16	362	648	5	43
Llanharan	26	1	0	25	277	1404	3	7

National Leagues
Division 1 East Champions: Bedlinog
Division 1 North Champions: Pwllheli
Division 1 West Champions: Dunvant

Women's Super Cup Finals
Cup Final
Skewen	54	Whitland	8

Plate Final
Ynysddu	12	Seven Sisters	15

Shield Final
Senghenydd	12	Porth Quins	10

Bowl Final
Ynysbwl	11	Gorseinon	5

Under 18 Final
Cardiff Quins	7	Whitland	10

IRELAND

Ulster Bank League Division 1A

	P	W	D	L	F	A	BP	Pts
Clontarf	18	13	2	3	413	280	8	64
Cork Constitution	18	10	2	6	424	279	12	56
Young Munster	18	12	2	4	345	327	4	56
UCD	18	9	1	8	434	330	9	47
Garryowen	18	7	2	9	290	359	8	40
Old Belvedere	18	8	0	10	323	361	6	38
Lansdowne	18	7	3	8	308	392	3	37
Terenure College	18	8	0	10	300	315	4	36
Ballynahinch	18	5	0	13	350	437	7	27
Galwegians	18	5	0	13	308	415	7	27

Ulster Bank League Division 1A Final
Clontarf 28 Cork Constitution 25

Ulster Bank League Division 1B

	P	W	D	L	F	A	BP	Pts
St Mary's College	18	16	0	2	461	278	8	72
Dublin University	18	14	0	4	516	264	14	70
Ballymena	18	11	0	7	448	344	10	54
Buccaneers	18	9	0	9	397	372	10	46
Old Wesley	18	8	0	10	385	417	12	44
Shannon	18	7	0	11	353	363	10	38
Dolphin	18	8	0	10	329	422	6	38
UL Bohemian	18	8	0	10	311	376	4	36
Blackrock College	18	6	0	12	323	461	8	32
Belfast 'Quins	18	3	0	15	287	513	7	19

Ulster Bank League Division 2A
Winners: Naas

Ulster Bank League Division 2B
Winners: Highfield

Ulster Bank League Division 2C
Winners: Old Crescent

Round Robin
Bangor	24	Westport	7
Enniscorthy	19	Bangor	19
Westport	0	Clonmel	38
Clonmel	7	Enniscorthy	22
Clonmel	12	Bangor	29
Enniscorthy	45	Westport	5

Winners: Bangor

Ulster Bank All Ireland Bateman Cup Final
Cork Constitution 38 Galwegians 19

All Ireland Junior Cup Final
Enniscorthy 23 Instonians 7

Fraser McMullen Cup Final
Cork Constitution 38 UCD 14

Women's All Ireland League Final
Old Belvedere 19 UL Bohemian 17

Women's All Ireland Cup Final
Cooke 7 Galwegians 10

GUINNESS PRO12 2015-16

	P	W	D	L	F	A	BP	Pts
Leinster	22	16	0	6	458	290	9	73
Connacht	22	15	0	7	507	406	13	73
Glasgow	22	14	1	7	557	380	14	72
Ulster	22	14	0	8	488	307	13	69
Scarlets	22	14	0	8	477	458	7	63
Munster	22	13	0	9	459	417	11	63
Blues	22	11	0	11	542	461	12	56
Ospreys	22	11	1	10	490	455	9	55
Edinburgh	22	11	0	11	405	366	10	54
Dragons	22	4	0	18	353	492	10	26
Zebre	22	5	0	17	308	718	4	24
Treviso	22	3	0	19	320	614	8	20

Guinness PRO12 Play-offs
Semi-finals
Leinster	30	Ulster	18
Connacht	16	Glasgow	11

Final
Connacht	20	Leinster	10

BRITISH & IRISH CUP 2015-16

Final
Yorkshire Carnegie 10 London Welsh 33

FRANCE

'Top 14' 2015-16 Play-offs

Semi-finals
Clermont Auvergne	33	Racing 92	34
Toulon	27	Montpellier	18

Final
Toulon	21	Racing 92	29

ITALY

Campionato Italiano d'Eccellenza 2015-16

Final
Femi-CZ Rovigo 20 Rugby Calvisano 13

EUROPEAN RUGBY CHAMPIONS CUP 2015-16

Quarter-finals

Saracens	29	Northampton	20
Wasps	25	Exeter	24
Racing 92	19	Toulon	16
Leicester	41	Stade Français	13

Semi-finals

Saracens	24	Wasps	17
Leicester	16	Racing 92	19

Final

Racing 92	9	Saracens	21

EUROPEAN RUGBY CHALLENGE CUP 2015-16

Quarter-finals

Harlequins	38	London Irish	30
Grenoble	33	Connacht	32
Sale	19	Montpellier	25
Gloucester	21	Dragons	23

Semi-finals

Harlequins	30	Grenoble	6
Montpellier	22	Dragons	12

Final

Harlequins	19	Montpellier	26

NEW ZEALAND

ITM Cup Premiership Final 2015

Canterbury	25	Auckland	23

ITM Cup Championship Final 2015

Hawke's Bay	26	Wellington	25

Heartland Champions 2015
Meads Cup: Wanganui
Lochore Cup: King Country

Ranfurly Shield holders: Waikato

SOUTH AFRICA

Currie Cup 2015
Final

Golden Lions	32	Western Province 24

SUPER RUGBY 2016

	P	W	D	L	F	A	BP	Pts
Hurricanes	15	11	0	4	458	314	9	53
Lions	15	11	0	4	535	349	8	52
Stormers	15	10	1	4	440	274	9	51
Brumbies	15	10	0	5	425	326	3	43
Highlanders	*15*	*11*	*0*	*4*	*422*	*273*	*8*	*52*
Chiefs	*15*	*11*	*0*	*4*	*491*	*341*	*7*	*51*
Crusaders	*15*	*11*	*0*	*4*	*487*	*317*	*6*	*50*
Sharks	15	9	1	5	360	269	5	43
Bulls	15	9	1	5	399	339	4	42
Waratahs	15	8	0	7	413	317	8	40
Blues	15	8	1	6	374	380	5	39
Rebels	15	7	0	8	365	486	3	31
Jaguares	15	4	0	11	376	427	6	22
Cheetahs	15	4	0	11	377	425	5	21
Reds	15	3	1	11	290	458	3	17
Force	15	2	0	13	260	441	5	13
Southern Kings	15	2	0	13	282	684	1	9
Sunwolves	15	1	1	13	293	627	3	9

Quarter-finals

Brumbies	9	Highlanders	15
Hurricanes	41	Sharks	0
Lions	42	Crusaders	25
Stormers	21	Chiefs	60

Semi-finals

Hurricanes	25	Chiefs	9
Lions	42	Highlanders	30

Final

Hurricanes	20	Lions	3

Key
Hurricanes: Conference winners
Highlanders: Wild Card teams

The table is for guidance only. The eight Super Rugby play-off places are decided on a conference/regional basis, with the four Conference winners making up positions one to four. The Wild Card teams, three from NZ/Aus and one from Africa, are the next best teams and make up positions five to eight.

BARBARIANS

Opponents	Results
Worcester	L 35-43
Gloucester	D 0-0
Argentina XV	L 31-49

Played 3 Drawn 1 Lost 2

Aberdeen
Simply asset management.

Aberdeen Asset
Management is proud
to support Wooden
Spoon, the children's
charity of rugby.

PREVIEW OF THE SEASON 2016-17

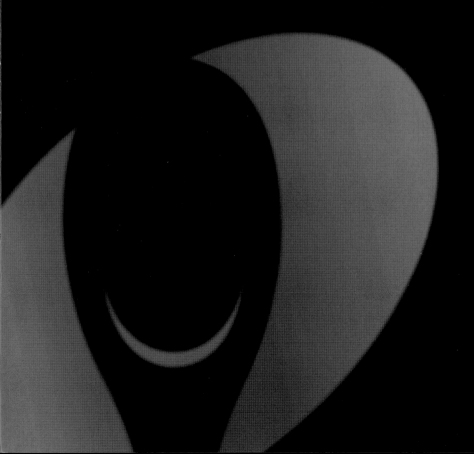

Key Players
selected by IAN ROBERTSON

ENGLAND

MANU TUILAGI
Leicester
Born: 18 May 1991
Height: 6ft Weight: 17st 4lbs
Centre – 26 caps (+1 Lions)
1st cap v Wales 2011

MARO ITOJE
Saracens
Born: 28 October 1994
Height: 6ft 5ins Weight: 18st 5lbs
Lock/back-row – 7 caps
1st cap v Italy 2016

SCOTLAND

DUNCAN TAYLOR
Saracens
Born: 5 September 1989
Height: 6ft 3ins Weight: 15st 6lbs
Wing/centre – 18 caps
1st cap v Samoa 2013

WP NEL
Edinburgh
Born: 30 April 1986
Height: 6ft Weight: 18st 12lbs
Prop – 15 caps
1st cap v Italy 2015

WALES

LIAM WILLIAMS
Scarlets
Born: 9 April 1991
Height: 6ft 1in Weight: 13st 12lbs
Full back/wing – 35 caps
1st cap v Barbarians 2012

JUSTIN TIPURIC
Ospreys
Born: 6 August 1989
Height: 6ft 2ins Weight: 15st 12lbs
Back-row – 43 caps (+1 Lions)
1st cap v Argentina 2011

Six Nations Championship

2016-17

IRELAND

CONOR MURRAY
Munster
Born: 20 April 1989
Height: 6ft 2ins Weight: 14st 10lbs
Scrum half – 50 caps (+2 Lions)
1st cap v France 2011

CJ STANDER
Munster
Born: 5 April 1990
Height: 6ft 1in Weight: 17st 13lbs
Back-row – 7 caps
1st cap v Wales 2016

FRANCE

JULES PLISSON
Stade Français
Born: 20 August 1991
Height: 6ft Weight: 13st 12lbs
Fly half – 13 caps
1st cap v England 2014

GUILHEM GUIRADO
Toulon
Born: 17 June 1986
Height: 5ft 11ins Weight: 16st 9lbs
Hooker – 43 caps
1st cap v Italy 2008

ITALY

TOMMASO ALLAN
Treviso
Born: 26 April 1993
Height: 6ft 1in Weight: 13st 9lbs
Fly half – 24 caps
1st cap v Australia 2013

JOSHUA FURNO
Newcastle
Born: 21 October 1989
Height: 6ft 6ins Weight: 17st
Lock – 36 caps
1st cap v Scotland 2011

Fixtures 2016-17

AUGUST 2016

Sat. 20th	AUSTRALIA v NZ (TRC/BC)
	SA v ARGENTINA (TRC)
Sat. 27th	NZ v AUSTRALIA (TRC/BC)
	ARGENTINA v SA (TRC)
	BT Scottish Premiership (1)
	BT Scottish Cup (1)

SEPTEMBER 2016

Fri. 2nd and Sat. 3rd	Guinness PRO12 (1)
Fri. 2nd to Sun. 4th	Aviva English Premiership (1)
Sat. 3rd	Greene King IPA Championship
	English National Leagues
	BT Scottish Premiership (2)
	BT Scottish National Leagues
	Welsh Principality Pr/ship (1)
	Welsh National Championship
	Welsh National Leagues
Fri 9th and Sat. 10th	Guinness PRO12 (2)
Fri. 9th to Sun. 11th	Aviva English Premiership (2)
Sat. 10th	NZ v ARGENTINA (TRC)
	AUSTRALIA v SA (TRC)
	English National Leagues
	BT Scottish Premiership (3)
	BT Scottish National Leagues
	Welsh Principality Pr/ship (2)
	Welsh National Championship
	Welsh National Leagues
	Welsh National Bowl (1)
Sat. 10th and Sun. 11th	Greene King IPA Championship
Fri. 16th and Sat. 17th	Guinness PRO12 (3)
	UB Irish Leagues
Fri. 16th to Sun. 18th	Aviva English Premiership (3)
Sat. 17th	NZ v SA (TRC/FC)
	AUSTRALIA v ARGENTINA (TRC)
	English National Leagues
	BT Scottish Premiership (4)
	BT Scottish National Leagues
	Welsh Principality Pr/ship (3)
	Welsh National Championship
	Welsh National Leagues
Sat. 17th and Sun. 18th	Greene King IPA Championship
Fri. 23rd and Sat. 24th	Guinness PRO12 (4)
	UB Irish Leagues
Fri. 23rd to Sun. 25th	Aviva English Premiership (4)
Sat. 24th	English National Leagues
	BT Scottish Premiership (5)
	BT Scottish National Leagues
	Welsh Principality Pr/ship (4)
	Welsh National Championship
	Welsh National Leagues
Sat. 24th and Sun. 25th	Greene King IPA Championship
Fri. 30th	BT Scottish National Leagues
	UB Irish Leagues 1A, 2A
Fri. 30th and Sat. 1st Oct.	Guinness PRO12 (5)
Fri. 30th to Sun. 2nd Oct.	Aviva English Premiership (5)

OCTOBER 2016

Sat. 1st	SA v AUSTRALIA (TRC/MCP)
	ARGENTINA v NZ (TRC)
	Greene King IPA Championship
	English National Leagues
	BT Scottish Premiership (6)
	Welsh Principality Pr/ship (5)
	Welsh National Championship
	Welsh National Leagues
	UB Irish Leagues
Fri. 7th and Sat. 8th	Guinness PRO12 (6)
Fri. 7th to Sun. 9th	Aviva English Premiership (6)
	UB Irish Leagues
Sat. 8th	SA v NZ (TRC/FC)
	ARGENTINA v AUSTRALIA (TRC – Twickenham)
	English National Leagues
	BT Scottish Premiership (7)
	BT Scottish National Leagues
	Welsh Principality Pr/ship (6)
	Welsh National Championship
	Welsh National Plate (1)
	Welsh National Bowl (2)
Sat. 8th and Sun. 9th	Greene King IPA Championship
Thu. 13th to Sun. 16th	European Champions Cup (1)
	European Challenge Cup (1)
Fri. 14th to Sun. 16th	British & Irish Cup (1)
Sat. 15th	English National Leagues
	BT Scottish Premiership (8)
	BT Scottish National Leagues
	Welsh National Championship
	Welsh National Leagues
Thu. 19th to Sun. 22nd	European Champions Cup (2)
	European Challenge Cup (2)
Fri. 21st.	BT Scottish National League 2
Sat. 22nd	NZ v AUSTRALIA (BC)
	English National Leagues
	BT Scottish Premiership (9)
	BT Scottish Nat Lges 1, 3
	Welsh National Championship

	Welsh National Leagues
	UB Irish League 2A
Sat. 22nd and	
Sun. 23rd	British & Irish Cup (2)
Fri. 28th and	
Sat. 29th	Guinness PRO12 (7)
	UB Irish Leagues
Fri. 28th to	
Sun. 30th	Aviva English Premiership (7)
Sat. 29th	Greene King IPA Championship
	BT Scottish Premiership (10)
	BT Scottish Nat Lges 1-3
	Welsh Principality Pr/ship (7)
	Welsh National Championship
	Welsh National Plate (2)
	Welsh National Bowl (3)

NOVEMBER 2016

Fri. 4th and	
Sat. 5th	Guinness PRO12 (8)
Fri. 4th to	
Sun. 6th	LV= (Anglo-Welsh) Cup
Sat. 5th	WALES v AUSTRALIA
	NZ v IRELAND
	(Soldier Field, Chicago)
	Barbarians v SA (Wembley)
	Greene King IPA Championship
	English National Leagues
	BT Scottish Premiership (11)
	BT Scottish National Leagues
	Welsh Principality Pr/ship (8)
	UB Irish Leagues
Fri. 11th	Barbarians v Fiji
	(Kingspan Stadium, Belfast)
Fri. 11th to	
Sun.13th	LV= (Anglo-Welsh) Cup
Sat. 12th	ENGLAND v SA
	SCOTLAND v AUSTRALIA
	FRANCE v SAMOA
	WALES v ARGENTINA
	IRELAND v CANADA
	ITALY v NZ
	English National Leagues
	Welsh Principality Pr/ship (9)
	Welsh National Championship
	Welsh National Leagues
	UB Irish Leagues
Fri. 18th	LV= (Anglo-Welsh) Cup
Fri. 18th to	
Sun. 20th	Aviva English Premiership (8)
Sat. 19th	ENGLAND v FIJI
	WALES v JAPAN
	SCOTLAND v ARGENTINA
	IRELAND v NZ
	FRANCE v AUSTRALIA
	ITALY v SA
	Greene King IPA Championship
	English National Leagues
	BT Scottish Cup (2)
	Welsh Principality Pr/ship (10)
Fri. 25th and	
Sat. 26th	UB Irish Leagues

Fri. 25th to	
Sun. 27th	Aviva English Premiership (9)
	Guinness PRO12 (9)
Sat. 26th	ENGLAND v ARGENTINA
	SCOTLAND v GEORGIA
	IRELAND v AUSTRALIA
	WALES v SA
	FRANCE v NZ
	ITALY v TONGA
	Greene King IPA Championship
	English National Leagues
	Welsh Principality Pr/ship (11)
	Welsh National Championship
	Welsh National Leagues

DECEMBER 2016

Fri. 2nd and	
Sat. 3rd	Guinness PRO12 (10)
Fri. 2nd to	
Sun. 4th	Aviva English Premiership (10)
Sat. 3rd	ENGLAND v AUSTRALIA
	English National Leagues
	BT Scottish Premiership (12)
	BT Scottish National Leagues
	Welsh Principality Pr/ship (12)
	Welsh National Championship
	Welsh National Leagues
	UB Irish Leagues 1A, 2A
Sat. 3rd and	Greene King IPA Championship
Sun. 4th	OU Women v CU Women 11:30
Thu. 8th	OU v CU 14:30
Thu. 8th to	
Sun. 11th	European Champions Cup (3)
	European Challenge Cup (3)
Sat. 10th and	
Sun. 11th	British & Irish Cup (3)
Sat. 10th	English National Leagues
	BT Scottish Premiership (13)
	BT Scottish National Leagues
	Welsh National Championship
	Welsh National Plate (3)
	Welsh National Bowl (4)
Thu. 15th to	
Sun. 18th	European Champions Cup (4)
	European Challenge Cup (4)
Fri. 16th	UB Irish League 1B
Fri. 16th to	
Sun. 18th	British & Irish Cup (4)
Sat. 17th	English National Leagues
	BT Scottish Premiership (14)
	BT Scottish National Leagues
	Welsh National Championship
	Welsh National Leagues
Fri. 23rd	Guinness PRO12 (11)
Fri. 23rd to	
Sun. 25th	Aviva English Premiership (11)
Sat. 24th	Greene King IPA Championship
	Welsh Principality Pr/ship (13)
Mon. 26th and	
Tue. 27th	Guinness PRO12 (11)
Sat. 31st	Greene King IPA Championship

Sat. 31st and	Welsh Principality Pr/ship (14)
Sun. 1st Jan.	Guinness PRO12 (12)
	Aviva English Premiership (12)

JANUARY 2017

Fri. 6th and	
Sat. 7th	Guinness PRO12 (13)
Sat. 7th	English National Leagues
	Welsh Principality Pr/ship (15)
	Welsh National Championship
	Welsh National Leagues
Sat. 7th and	
Sun. 8th	Aviva English Premiership (13)
Thu. 12th to	
Sun. 15th	European Champions Cup (5)
	European Challenge Cup (5)
Fri. 13th to	
Sun. 15th	British & Irish Cup (5)
Sat. 14th	English National Leagues
	BT Scottish Premiership (15)
	BT Scottish National Leagues
	Welsh National Championship
	Welsh National Plate (4)
	Welsh National Bowl (5)
	UB Irish League 2A
Thu. 19th to	
Sun. 22nd	European Champions Cup (6)
	European Challenge Cup (6)
Sat. 21st	British & Irish Cup (6)
	English National Leagues
	BT Scottish Premiership (16)
	BT Scottish National Leagues
	Welsh National Championship
	Welsh National Leagues
	UB Irish League 2A
Thu. 26th to	
Sun. 29th	LV= (Anglo-Welsh) Cup
Sat. 28th	Greene King IPA Championship
	English National Leagues
	Welsh National Leagues
	Welsh National Cup (1)
	UB Irish Leagues
Sat. 28th and	
Sun. 29th	BT Scottish Cup (3)

FEBRUARY 2017

Fri. 3rd and	
Sat. 4th	UB Irish Leagues
Sat. 4th	SCOTLAND v IRELAND 14:25
	ENGLAND v FRANCE 16:50
	English National Leagues
	+Welsh Principality Pr/ship (i)
	Welsh National Championship
	Welsh National Leagues
Sat. 4th and	
Sun. 5th	LV= (Anglo-Welsh) Cup
	Greene King IPA Championship
Sun. 5th	ITALY v WALES 14:00
Fri. 10th	Guinness PRO12 (14)
Fri. 10th and	

Sat. 11th	Aviva English Premiership (14)
	UB Irish Leagues
Sat. 11th	ITALY v IRELAND 14:25
	WALES v ENGLAND 16:50
	English National Leagues
	BT Scottish Premiership (17)
	BT Scottish National Leagues
	+Welsh Principality Pr/ship (ii)
Sun. 12th	FRANCE v SCOTLAND 15:00
Fri. 17th	Guinness PRO12 (15)
Fri. 17th to	
Sun. 19th	Aviva English Premiership (15)
Sat. 18th	English National Leagues
	BT Scottish Premiership (18)
	BT Scottish National Leagues
	Welsh National Leagues
	Welsh National Cup (2)
	Welsh National Plate (5)
	Welsh National Bowl (6)
	UB Irish Leagues
Fri. 24th	Guinness PRO12 (16)
Fri. 24th to	
Sun. 26th	Aviva English Premiership (16)
Sat. 25th and	
Sun. 26th	Greene King IPA Championship
Sat. 25th	SCOTLAND v WALES 14:25
	IRELAND v FRANCE 16:50
	+Welsh Principality Pr/ship (iii)
Sun. 26th	ENGLAND v ITALY 15:00

MARCH 2017

Fri. 3rd and	
Sat. 4th	UB Irish Leagues
Fri. 3rd to	
Sun. 5th	Guinness PRO12 (17)
	Aviva English Premiership (17)
Sat. 4th	English National Leagues
	BT Scottish National Leagues
	BT Scottish Cup QF
	Welsh National Championship
	Welsh National Leagues
	Welsh National Cup (3)
	Welsh National Plate (6)
	Welsh National Bowl (7)
Sat. 4th and	
Sun. 5th	Green King IPA Championship
Fri. 10th	WALES v IRELAND 20:05
Fri. 10th to	
Sun. 12th	British & Irish Cup QF
Sat. 11th	ITALY v FRANCE 13:30
	ENGLAND v SCOTLAND 16:00
	LV= (Anglo-Welsh) Cup SF
	English National Leagues
	BT Scottish National Leagues
	Welsh National Championship
	Welsh National Leagues
	UB Irish Leagues
Sat. 18th	SCOTLAND v ITALY 12:30
	FRANCE v WALES 14:45
	IRELAND v ENGLAND 17:00
	Greene King IPA Championship

+Welsh Principality Pr/ship (iv)

Fri. 24th to
Sun. 26th   Guinness PRO12 (18)
Sat. 25th   English National Leagues
    BT Scottish National Leagues
    BT Scottish Cup SF
    BT Scottish Shield SF
    BT Scottish Bowl SF
    Welsh National Leagues
    Welsh National Cup SF
    Welsh National Plate SF
    Welsh National Bowl SF
    UB Irish Leagues

Sat. 25th and
Sun. 26th   Aviva English Premiership (18)
    Greene King IPA Championship
Wed. 29th   NatWest Schools Cups Finals
Thu. 30th   *BUCS/AASE Finals
Thu. 30th to
Sun. 2nd Apr.   *European Champions Cup QF
    *European Challenge Cup QF

Fri. 31st to
Sun. 2nd Apr.   *British & Irish Cup SF

APRIL 2017
Sat. 1st   English National Leagues
    BT Scottish National Leagues
    Welsh National Championship
    Welsh National Leagues

Fri. 7th to
Sun. 9th   Guinness PRO12 (19)
    Aviva English Premiership (19)
    UB Irish Leagues
Sat. 8th   St George's Day Game
    Greene King IPA Championship
    +Welsh Principality Pr/ship (v)
    Welsh National Leagues

Fri. 14th and
Sat. 15th   Guinness PRO12 (20)
Sat. 15th   Greene King IPA Championship
    English National Leagues
    Welsh National Leagues
    **BT Scottish Cup Final
    **BT Scottish Shield Final
    **BT Scottish Bowl Final
    UB Irish Leagues

Sat. 15th and
Sun. 16th   Aviva English Premiership (20)
Sun. 16th   Welsh National Cup Final
    Welsh National Plate Final
    Welsh National Bowl Final

Fri. 21st to
Sun. 23rd   *European Champions Cup SF
    *European Challenge Cup SF
Sat. 22nd   British & Irish Cup Final
    English National Leagues

Fri. 28th and
Sat. 29th   Aviva English Premiership (21)
Fri. 28th to
Sun. 30th   Guinness PRO12 (21)
    *GKIPA Championship SF (1)
Sat. 29th   Army v Navy (Twickenham)

English National Leagues
English Nat Lges/Divisional
    Play-offs
+Welsh Principality Pr/ship (vi)

MAY 2017
Fri. 5th to
Sun. 7th   *GKIPA Championship SF (2)
Sat. 6th   Guinness PRO12 (22)
    Aviva English Premiership (22)
    Welsh Principality Pr/ship (vii)
    English Nat Lge 1 & 2 Play-off
    RFU Intermediate Cup Final
    RFU Senior Vase Final
    RFU Junior Vase Final
    English National U20 Cup Final
Fri. 12th   European Challenge Cup Final
    (venue TBC)
Sat. 13th   European Champions Cup Final
    (Murrayfield)
w/c 13th   GKIPA Championship Final (1)
Fri. 19th and
Sat. 20th   *Aviva English Premiership SF
Fri. 19th to
Sun. 21st   *Guinness PRO12 SF
w/c 20th   GKIPA Championship Final (2)
Sat. 20th and
Sun. 21st   HSBC 7s WS (London)
Sat. 27th   Guinness PRO12 Final
    Aviva English Premiership Final
Sun. 28th   ENGLAND v TBC (Twickenham)
    English Cty Ch/ship Final
    (Bill Beaumont Cup)
    English Cty Ch/ship Plate Final
    English Cty Ch/ship Shield Final

Key
TRC = The Rugby Championship
BC = Bledisloe Cup
FC = Freedom Cup
MCP = Mandela Challenge Plate
*dates and times to be confirmed
** date and time of final to be confirmed
+ the Welsh Principality Premiership will now
play in a league of 16 teams for the first half of
the season. It will then split into two divisions,
the top teams of each then playing off for the
title. Play-off dates to be announced.

JUNE/JULY 2017
British & Irish Lions Tour to New Zealand

Sat.	3rd June	v Prov. Union XV (Whangarei)
Wed.	7th	v Blues (Auckland)
Sat.	10th	v Crusaders (Christchurch)
Tue.	13th	v Highlanders (Dunedin)
Sat.	17th	v Maori All Blacks (Rotorua)
Tue.	20th	v Chiefs (Hamilton)
Sat.	24th	v NEW ZEALAND (Auckland)
Tue.	27th	v Hurricanes (Wellington)
Sat.	1st July	v NEW ZEALAND (Wellington)
Sat.	8th	v NEW ZEALAND (Auckland)